# Living
## in
# Christ

A Study of Luther's Small Catechism

## Originally prepared by
## The Synodical Catechism Committee, 1948

### Revised 2004

CONCORDIA PUBLISHING HOUSE · SAINT LOUIS

with you and that you may enjoy long life on the earth."
**Eph. 6:1–3**

## To Workers of All Kinds

Slaves, obey your earthly masters with respect and fear, and with sincerity of heart, just as you would obey Christ. Obey them not only to win their favor when their eye is on you, but like slaves of Christ, doing the will of God from your heart. Serve wholeheartedly, as if you were serving the Lord, not men, because you know that the Lord will reward everyone for whatever good he does, whether he is slave or free. **Eph. 6:5–8**

## To Employers and Supervisors

Masters, treat your slaves in the same way. Do not threaten them, since you know that he who is both their Master and yours is in heaven, and there is no favoritism with Him. **Eph. 6:9**

## To Youth

Young men, in the same way be submissive to those who are older. All of you, clothe yourselves with humility toward one another, because, "God opposes the proud but gives grace to the humble." Humble yourselves, therefore, under God's mighty hand, that He may lift you up in due time. **1 Peter 5:5–6**

## To Widows

The widow who is really in need and left all alone puts her hope in God and continues night and day to pray and to ask God for help. But the widow who lives for pleasure is dead even while she lives. **1 Tim. 5:5–6**

## To Everyone

The commandments . . . are summed up in this one rule: "Love your neighbor as yourself." **Rom. 13:9**

I urge . . . that requests, prayers, intercession and thanksgiving be made for everyone. **1 Tim. 2:1**

*Let each his lesson learn with care,*
*And all the household well shall fare.*

# Christian Questions
with Their Answers

PREPARED BY DR. MARTIN LUTHER FOR THOSE
WHO INTEND TO GO TO THE SACRAMENT

After confession and instruction in the Ten Commandments, the Creed, the Lord's Prayer, and the Sacraments of Baptism and the Lord's Supper, the pastor may ask, or Christians may ask themselves these questions:

1. *Do you believe that you are a sinner?*
   Yes, I believe it. I am a sinner.
2. *How do you know this?*
   From the Ten Commandments, which I have not kept.
3. *Are you sorry for your sins?*
   Yes, I am sorry that I have sinned against God.
4. *What have you deserved from God because of your sins?*
   His wrath and displeasure, temporal death, and eternal damnation. See **Romans 6:21, 23**.
5. *Do you hope to be saved?*
   Yes, that is my hope.
6. *In whom then do you trust?*
   In my dear Lord Jesus Christ.
7. *Who is Christ?*
   The Son of God, true God and man.

\* The "Christian Questions with Their Answers," designating Luther as the author, first appeared in an edition of the Small Catechism in 1551.

8. *How many Gods are there?*
   Only one, but there are three persons: Father, Son, and Holy Spirit.

9. *What has Christ done for you that you trust in Him?*
   He died for me and shed His blood for me on the cross for the forgiveness of sins.

10. *Did the Father also die for you?*
    He did not. The Father is God only, as is the Holy Spirit; but the Son is both true God and true man. He died for me and shed his blood for me.

11. *How do you know this?*
    From the holy Gospel, from the words instituting the Sacrament, and by His body and blood given me as a pledge in the Sacrament.

12. *What are the Words of Institution?*
    Our Lord Jesus Christ, on the night when He was betrayed, took bread and when He had given thanks, He broke it and gave it to the disciples and said: "Take eat; this is My body, which is given for you. This do in remembrance of Me."
    In the same way also He took the cup after supper, and when He had given thanks, He gave it to them, saying: "Drink of it, all of you; this cup is the new testament in My blood, which is shed for you for the forgiveness of sins. This do, as often as you drink it, in remembrance of Me."

13. *Do you believe, then, that the true body and blood of Christ are in the Sacrament?*
    Yes, I believe it.

14. *What convinces you to believe this?*
    The word of Christ: Take, eat, this is My body; drink of it, all of you, this is My blood.

15. *What should we do when we eat His body and drink His blood, and in this way receive His pledge?*
    We should remember and proclaim His death and the shedding of His blood, as He taught us: This do, as often as you drink it, in remembrance of Me.

16. *Why should we remember and proclaim His death?*
    First, so that we may learn to believe that no creature could make satisfaction for our sins. Only Christ, true

God and man, could do that. Second, so we may learn to be horrified by our sins, and to regard them as very serious. Third, so we may find joy and comfort in Christ alone, and through faith in Him be saved.

17. *What motivated Christ to die and make full payment for your sins?*
His great love for His Father and for me and other sinners, as it is written in **John 14**; **Romans 5**; **Galatians 2** and **Ephesians 5**.

18. *Finally, why do you wish to go to the Sacrament?*
That I may learn to believe that Christ, out of great love, died for my sin, and also learn from Him to love God and my neighbor.

19. *What should admonish and encourage a Christian to receive the Sacrament frequently?*
First, both the command and the promise of Christ the Lord. Second, his own pressing need, because of which the command, encouragement, and promise are given.

20. *But what should you do if you are not aware of this need and have no hunger and thirst for the Sacrament?*
To such a person no better advice can be given than this: first, he should touch his body to see if he still has flesh and blood. Then he should believe what the Scriptures say of it in **Galatians 5** and **Romans 7**. Second, he should look around to see whether he is still in the world, and remember that there will be no lack of sin and trouble, as the Scriptures say in **John 15–16** and in **1 John 2** and **5**. Third, he will certainly have the devil also around him, who with his lying and murdering day and night will let him have no peace, within or without, as the Scriptures picture him in **John 8** and **16**; **1 Peter 5**; **Ephesians 6**; and **2 Timothy 2**.

## NOTE

These questions and answers are no child's play, but are drawn up with great earnestness of purpose by the venerable and devout Dr. Luther for both young and old. Let each one pay attention and consider it a serious matter; for St. Paul writes to the Galatians in chapter six: "Do not be deceived: God cannot be mocked."

## PART TWO

## *UNIT 1* The Existence of God

*I Believe in God*

# HOW WE LEARN ABOUT GOD

There is a God. Every Christian believes there is a God and that Jesus Christ is God's Son and our Savior. Many other people who have never seen a Bible also know there is a supreme being. This is not surprising, because God has revealed some information about Himself through the things He has created.

The sun, moon, and stars in the sky, beautiful by day and by night, along with the mysteries of the universe that scientists are exploring, point us to God. The earth, with its variety of lovely and useful plants and minerals, reminds us of God. Thousands of living creatures, all of them wonderfully made, proclaim that there is a God. The intricacies and magnificence of everything in nature are evidence that a supreme being exists.

Every house has a builder; every watch has a maker; every book has an author. In a similar way, this world has a Maker, a Creator, who made the whole world and still preserves it. Christians believe that something so magnificent as the universe could never happen by chance or accident; it could not evolve from simpler units.

We also learn about God through a voice within us called our conscience. Our conscience warns us that some things we might think about or do are wrong. Knowledge of these wrongful actions is placed in our hearts by our Creator, God. Our conscience tells us that there is someone higher than we are to whom we must answer for our deeds.

Some people, called atheists, believe that there is no God. God continues to love these people. He wants us to proclaim the Good News of His forgiving love, shown in sending His Son to be the redeemer of all people, so that they, too, can be saved (1 Timothy 2:4).

What can be learned about God from nature and from our conscience does not give a complete picture of who God is. Only from the Bible can we get the most complete picture of God. In the Bible God Himself tells us exactly who He is and what He has done for us through Jesus Christ, God's Son and our Savior.

## QUESTIONS FOR DISCUSSION

**1. What does nature tell us about God?**

**2. What does your conscience tell you about God?**

**3. Where can you learn the full truth about God?**

# Bible Readings

God is spirit. John 4:24

No one has ever seen God, but God the One and Only, who is at the Father's side, has made Him known. John 1:18

From everlasting to everlasting You are God. Psalm 90:2

I the LORD do not change. Malachi 3:6

For nothing is impossible with God. Luke 1:37

Lord, You know all things. John 21:17

"Do not I fill heaven and earth?" declares the Lord. Jeremiah 23:24

I, the LORD, your God, am holy. Leviticus 19:2

The LORD is good to all; He has compassion on all He has made. Psalm 145:9

God is love. 1 John 4:8

# Bible Teachings

God is the highest being in existence. The almighty God is far above heaven and earth, yet He is near me at all times. God is without beginning and without end, always the same. I cannot see God, because God has no body. He is a spirit. At the same time, He is a personal being with a mind and a will. Even though I cannot see Him, I can know Him through His Word.

*The Chi-Rho is an early monogram for Christ. It is made of the first two letters in the Greek word for Christ.*

God can do anything He pleases. He knows everything. He is everywhere in heaven and earth at the same time; therefore I am never alone. God is a perfect being, without sin. He keeps His promises.

One of the most wonderful truths about God is that He is kind to all His creatures. He loves me. He uses His wisdom and power for my good. He knows all my troubles and helps me in every need, no matter where I may be.

# QUESTIONS AND ANSWERS

**1. Who is the highest being?**
God is the highest being.

**2. How do we know there is a God?**
Nature, which did not create itself, tells us
A voice within us (conscience) tells us
The Bible tells us
} there is a God.

**3. Why can't we see God?**
We can't see God because God is a spirit.

**4. What is a spirit?**
A spirit is a being that has a mind and a will but is without a body.

**5. How does the Bible describe God?**
The Bible tells us that God is eternal, unchangeable, almighty, all-knowing, everywhere present, holy, just, faithful, benevolent, merciful, and gracious. These are some of His attributes.

**6. Why do you believe that God is eternal?**
Psalm 90:2 says, "From everlasting to everlasting You are God" (eternal).

**7. Why is it always safe to trust God and His works?**
God does not change; He remains the same all the time (unchangeable).

**8. How great is the power of God?**
God is almighty; He can help me in every trouble (omnipotent).

**9. Why can nothing be hidden from God?**
God knows all things, even our most secret thoughts (omniscient).

10. **Where is God?**
    God is everywhere; He is always with me (omnipresent).

11. **Why is it impossible for God to do anything wrong?**
    God is holy; He loves good and hates evil (holy).

12. **How does God show that He is a just God?**
    God is fair in His dealings with all people (just).

13. **Why can we believe that God will always do what He says?**
    God has been faithful in the past; He has kept His promises and carried out His judgments (faithful).

14. **How does God feel toward all His creatures?**
    God is loving and kind; He wants only what is good for His creatures (benevolent).

15. **What comfort do we get from knowing that God is merciful?**
    We are sure that He will abundantly pardon all who are sorry for their sins and believe in Jesus as their Savior (merciful).

16. **Why do Christians give all glory to God?**
    God is gracious; He blesses us richly in Christ, even though we do not deserve His blessings or the forgiveness He gives us through Jesus (gracious).

# WORD STUDY

*abundantly:* richly; plentifully

*conscience:* a voice within us that urges us to do what is right and warns us against what is wrong

*grace:* God's undeserved love for all people

*to pardon:* to forgive

*to preserve:* to uphold

*salvation:* giving freedom and life to one imprisoned by sin and death

# HYMN STANZA

Sing praise to God, the highest good,
The Author of creation,
The God of love who understood
Our need for His salvation.
With healing balm our souls He fills
And ev'ry faithless murmur stills:
To God all praise and glory!

*LW* 452:1

# PRAYER

Almighty and everlasting God, I thank You that You have made Yourself known to me. I beg You, bless my study of Your Word, that by Your grace I may know, honor, and praise You all my life. Through Jesus Christ, Your Son and my Savior, I pray. Amen.

# WHAT THIS MEANS TO ME

How comforting it is for me to know that at all times and in all places the holy, almighty God is always at my side and cares for me with an everlasting love! With Him close to me, I know that all things will work together for my good. I know that God loves me, because He has told me so in His holy book, the Bible.

# UNIT 2

## The Triune God

*In the Name of the Father
and of the Son and of the Holy Spirit*

## BIBLE STORY

### The Baptism of Jesus

Matthew 3:13–17

Near the Jordan River something exciting was taking place. Dressed in a robe made of camel's hair, a man was preaching with great power. People from all over Palestine hurried out to hear him. "Repent!" he called. "Be truly sorry for your sins. The kingdom of God is here. Be baptized for the forgiveness of your sins."

"Could this be the promised Messiah, who will set up the kingdom of God?" the people asked.

This man was not the Messiah. He was John the Baptist. "I am only the forerunner of the Messiah," he said. "God has sent me to prepare the way for the Lord Christ." Day after day people from all walks of life came to hear John preach. He baptized many of them.

One day Jesus came and asked to be baptized. Even though He is the holy Son of God, He stood humbly with the lost, the least, and the lowest. He wanted to save them all from sin and bring them into His loving Father's family.

When he saw Jesus, John the Baptist exclaimed, "I need to be baptized by You, and yet You come to me!"

Jesus answered, "Let it be this way for now. I must fulfill all righteousness."

Satisfied with Jesus' answer, John baptized Him.

As Jesus came up from the river's edge—wonder of wonders!—the heavens opened, and the Holy Spirit came down upon Jesus in the form of a dove. At the same time a voice from heaven called out, "This is My beloved Son. I am pleased with Him."

## QUESTIONS FOR DISCUSSION

**1. Why did John baptize Jesus?**

**2. Identify where the three persons of the Holy Trinity are present in this biblical event.**

**3. What words did the pastor use when he baptized you? Why does he use these words?**

## BIBLE READINGS

Hear, O Israel: The LORD our God, the LORD is one. Deuteronomy 6:4

There is no God but one. 1 Corinthians 8:4

May the grace of the Lord Jesus Christ, and the love of God, and the fellowship of the Holy Spirit be with you all. 2 Corinthians 13:14

Go and make disciples of all nations, baptizing them in the name of the Father and of the Son and of the Holy Spirit. Matthew 28:19

All may honor the Son just as they honor the Father. John 5:23

## BIBLE TEACHINGS

Our God is a wonderful God. He is beyond our understanding. He is one being, undivided. There is no being like Him.

Yet God is three distinct persons, Father, Son, and Holy Spirit. The Father is true God; the Son is true God; the Holy Spirit is true God. Nevertheless, there are not three Gods, but only one God. Because there are three persons in God, we call God the triune God, or the Holy Trinity.

I cannot fully understand the Trinity, but I believe this teaching because God Himself has revealed His nature to me in the Bible. This doctrine brings me joy because it assures me that all three persons in God work together for my eternal happiness, as my Creator, my Redeemer, and my Sanctifier.

# QUESTIONS AND ANSWERS

**1. Who is the only true God?**

The only true God is the triune God, or the Holy Trinity.

**2. What is the Holy Trinity?**

The Holy Trinity is three distinct persons in one God. Each person in the Trinity possesses the power and glory of God equally. Even though there are three persons in the Trinity, there is only one God.

**3. Who are the three persons in God?**

The three persons in God are the Father, the Son, and the Holy Spirit.

**4. Who is the Father?**

The Father is God and is called the First Person of the Holy Trinity. The Father is primarily associated with the work of creation.

**5. Who is the Son?**

The Son is God and is called the Second Person of the Holy Trinity. The Son is primarily associated with the work of redemption.

**6. Who is the Holy Spirit?**

The Holy Spirit is God and is called the Third Person of the Holy Trinity. The Holy Spirit is primarily associated with the work of sanctification.

**7. Why do you believe the doctrine of the Holy Trinity?**

I believe this doctrine because God's Word, the Bible, teaches it.

**8. Why is it important to believe in the triune God?**

The triune God is the only true God; only those who believe in Him have eternal life.

# WORD STUDY

*Sanctifier:* the Holy Spirit, who makes us holy by creating our faith in Christ

*Creator:* Maker, a name usually used for God the Father

*Holy Trinity:* Father, Son, and Holy Spirit—three in one

*Messiah:* Christ, or the anointed Savior

*Redeemer:* Savior, the One who buys us back from Satan

*triune:* three in one

*doctrine:* a teaching of the church based on the Bible

*righteousness:* acting according to God's commands

THREE IN ONE — ONE IN THREE — Father — Son — God — Holy Spirit

# HYMN STANZA

Holy, holy, holy! Lord God Almighty!
All Thy works shall praise Thy name in earth and sky and sea.
Holy, holy, holy, merciful and mighty!
God in three Persons, blessed Trinity!

*LW* 168:4

## PRAYER

Dear Lord, You have made Yourself known to me as the triune God, Father, Son, and Holy Spirit. Keep me faithful to You throughout my life and help me to confess to others that You are the one true God; who lives and reigns forever. Amen.

## WHAT THIS MEANS TO ME

I know that all three persons in the triune God, Father, Son, and Holy Spirit, work constantly for my eternal happiness. In thankfulness to God and by the power of the Holy Spirit that is given to me, I will faithfully worship, trust, and serve my God with my whole self throughout my life.

# UNIT 3

*Your Word Is True*

The Bible

## BIBLE STORY

### Timothy's Boyhood Training

2 Timothy 1:1–5; 3:14–17

In Lystra lived a fine, godly boy by the name of Timothy. When he was still a little child, his mother and grandmother told him the wonderful Bible stories that so many people know and love.

From these stories Timothy learned about God. He learned that God created the world. He learned about how God has dealt with His people, such as Abraham, Isaac, Jacob, Joseph, Moses, David, and many others.

Timothy learned especially that all people are sinners. He learned that many times God promised to one day send a Savior to save His people from suffering the punishment for their sin.

When Timothy grew to be a young man, the

apostle Paul visited his home. Paul told him about Jesus. Paul told him that Jesus fulfilled all of God's promises about the Savior. Timothy believed in Jesus with all his heart and made up his mind to become a pastor. Paul loved him as if he were his own son.

Later, when they lived in different towns, Paul wrote Timothy two letters. These letters are included in the Bible. To explain to Timothy why the Scriptures were so valuable, Paul wrote in his second letter, "From infancy you have known the holy Scriptures, which are able to make you wise for salvation through faith in Christ Jesus" (2 Timothy 3:15).

The letter continues, "All Scripture is God-breathed and is useful for teaching, rebuking, correcting and training in righteousness, so that the man of God may be thoroughly equipped for every good work" (2 Timothy 3:15–17).

## QUESTIONS FOR DISCUSSION

**1. Where did Timothy's mother and grandmother find the stories they taught him?**

**2. What were the main truths Timothy learned?**

**3. From whom did Timothy hear about his Savior, Jesus?**

**4. What may we learn about the Bible from this story?**

## BIBLE READINGS

This is what the LORD, the God of Israel, says. Joshua 24:2

[God] said [this] through His holy prophets of long ago. Luke 1:70

Men spoke from God as they were carried along by the Holy Spirit. 2 Peter 1:21

We speak . . . in words taught by the Spirit.
1 Corinthians 2:13

All Scripture is God-breathed. 2 Timothy 3:16

The Scripture cannot be broken. John 10:35

Your Word is truth. John 17:17

The holy Scriptures . . . are able to make you wise for salvation through faith in Christ Jesus. 2 Timothy 3:15

Your Word is a lamp to my feet and a light for my path. Psalm 119:105

Blessed . . . are those who hear the Word of God and obey it. Luke 11:28

## BIBLE TEACHINGS

*Your Word is truth.*

The Bible, or Holy Scripture, is the Word of God. Many men of God wrote it, but God gave them the thoughts and the words to write. Every word comes from God. Therefore every word is true.

The part of the Bible that was written before the birth of Jesus is called the Old Testament. The part that was written after the birth of Jesus is called the New Testament.

In the Bible God tells me about Himself and about His creation of the world and the first people. God also tells about the origin of sin. Sin is the transgression, or breaking, of God's Law (actual sin); it is also the wicked condition of people since Adam's and Eve's fall into sin (original sin).

The most wonderful truth God tells me in the Bible is that, because of His great love for me, He gave His Son, Jesus, to be my Savior from sin. This wonderful message that there is forgiveness for sin and salvation for all through Jesus is called the Gospel.

God also tells me in His Word how He wants me to live here on earth. God wants me to study His Word, to believe the Gospel, to love it dearly, and to follow it all my life. When I live according to His Word in thankfulness for His love, I will be greatly blessed.

## QUESTIONS AND ANSWERS

1. **Which is the most important book for people to read and study?**
   The Bible (the Holy Scriptures) is the most important book because it reveals to us God's message of salvation through Jesus.

2. **Why is the Bible the best and most important book?**
   The Bible is the Word of God, which tells us we were saved through Jesus' suffering, death, and resurrection.

3. **Who wrote the Bible?**
   Many men of God wrote the Bible.

4. **How can the Bible be the Word of God if it was written by men?**
   The Bible is the Word of God because God gave these men the thoughts and the words to write.

5. **How much of the Bible was given or inspired by God?**
   "All Scripture is God-breathed" (2 Timothy 3:16).

6. **What must we therefore say of every word in the Bible?**
   Since God gave us the Scriptures, every word in the Bible is true and dependable. This teaching is called the doctrine of verbal inspiration.

7. **For what purpose did God give us His Word?**
   God gave us His Word so that we might learn that He has given us salvation through His Son. His Word also gives us guidance for living a godly life.

8. **What is the most important doctrine, or teaching, of the Bible?**

The teaching that Jesus is my Savior is the most important doctrine of the Bible.

9. **Which part of the Bible was written before the birth of Jesus?**

The Old Testament was written before the birth of Jesus.

10. **Which part of the Bible was written after the birth of Jesus?**

The New Testament was written after the birth of Jesus.

11. **How does God want us to use the Bible?**

God wants us to study the Bible daily, to believe its message of salvation through Jesus, to use it to guide our prayer life, to trust it as a guide for living lives pleasing to God, and to honor and respect it as His Word to us.

## WORD STUDY

*divine:* belonging to God

*correction:* act of making better

*inspiration:* the action of the Holy Spirit giving the writers of Scripture the words and thoughts to write

*reproof:* the act of blaming or condemning as wrong

## HYMN STANZA

How precious is the book divine,
By inspiration giv'n!
Bright as a lamp its teachings shine
To guide our souls to heav'n.

*LW* 332:1

# PRAYER

Blessed Lord, You have given the Bible to teach me the way to heaven. Help me love to read and study Your Word so that my faith in Jesus as my Savior will be strong. Send Your Holy Spirit to me so that I may gladly hear and learn Your Word. May Your Word be a lamp to my feet and a light to my path. Through Jesus Christ, my Savior, I pray. Amen.

# WHAT THIS MEANS TO ME

I know the Holy Spirit will help me love to hear and study God's holy Word, the Bible. Strengthened by the Spirit, I will pay attention when it is taught, study it on my own and with others, and follow its teaching in my everyday life. I know that through God's Word I will not only receive God's blessings for my earthly life, but I will also be brought closer to Jesus, who is the way to eternal joy in heaven.

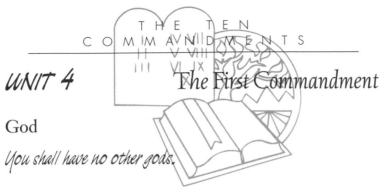

# UNIT 4      The First Commandment

## God

*You shall have no other gods.*

*What does this mean?*

We should fear, love, and trust in God above all things.

## BIBLE STORY

### The Giving of the Law      Exodus 19–20

East of the Red Sea is the Sinai peninsula. It is rugged, barren country. Rising above the desert towers a steep mountain. This is Mount Sinai. Looking at the drowsy quiet that hangs over the mountain and the surrounding wilderness, one would never imagine that anything of importance to us ever happened there.

Yet, about 3,500 years ago, more than a million freed slaves crowded around Mount Sinai to take part in one of the greatest happenings in the history of the world. From the mountaintop came the voice of God Himself. "I am the LORD your God, who brought you out of Egypt, out of the land of slavery," God said (Deuteronomy 5:6). These words were a friendly greeting from the Lord of heaven and earth to His chosen

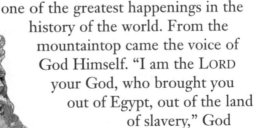

people. He wanted them to love Him and be glad to do His will.

And well they might! In these words God was saying to them, "Remember how good I have been to you! I have delivered you from a long time of Egyptian slavery. I have *proven* to you that I am your God, your Friend and Helper. Now have Me as your God. Worship Me and no other god. Do not bow down to the gods of the unbelievers about you."

While the earth shook, thunder rolled, lightning flashed, and smoke blocked out the mountain, God gave His people the Ten Commandments. In them He made known His holy will to the people of Israel. Then God wrote the Ten Commandments on two tablets of stone that Moses was to give to the people. Later God commanded Moses to write His instructions in a book. This book of Moses has been divided into the first five books of the Bible. From the Bible all people can know God's holy will and receive strength to obey it.

## QUESTIONS FOR DISCUSSION

1. **Which people gathered around Mount Sinai about 3,500 years ago?**

2. **Before He gave His people the Ten Commandments, what did God want them to remember?**

3. **Read the Ten Commandments in Exodus 20.**

4. **State the meaning of each commandment in your own words. Who makes known His will in the Ten Commandments?**

5. **Why should you know the Ten Commandments?**

# Bible Readings

Worship the Lord your God, and serve Him only. Matthew 4:10

I am the Lord; that is My name! I will not give My glory to another or My praise to idols. Isaiah 42:8

Anyone who loves his father or mother more than Me is not worthy of Me; anyone who loves his son or daughter more than Me is not worthy of Me. Matthew 10:37

To fear the Lord is to hate evil. Proverbs 8:13

Love the Lord your God with all your heart and with all your soul and with all your mind. Matthew 22:37

It is better to take refuge in the Lord than to trust in man. Psalm 118:8

# Bible Teachings

*Love the Lord*

The only true God is the triune God: Father, Son, and Holy Spirit. God deserves the first place in our heart, for He is our most faithful friend. He alone is to be worshiped.

If we worship any other god or place anything else as most important in our lives, we are worshiping an idol and are sinning against the First Commandment. We commit this sin also if we fear any creature more than God or if we love our parents, money, food, friends, good times, or anything else more than we love God and His Word. We also commit this sin when we trust anyone or anything more than we trust God. *Whatever is most important in our lives is really our god.*

The First Commandment summarizes all of the commandments. If we could keep this one by loving and honoring God perfectly, we would automatically be keeping all the others. When we fear the Lord above all things, we do no evil; when we love Him above all things, we serve Him only; when we trust in Him above all things, we trust Him in all things.

God wants me to be perfect in all things, especially in keeping this commandment. When I fail, I know that He forgives me for Jesus' sake.

## QUESTIONS AND ANSWERS

**1. Who is the God to be worshiped by everyone?**
The triune God, Father, Son, and Holy Spirit, is the true God that we are to worship.

**2. Why should we worship only the triune God?**
Only the triune God gives us life and happiness, the joys of earth, and the hope of heaven through Jesus, our Savior.

**3. How should we worship God?**
To worship the true God, we fear, love, and trust in Him above all things.

**4. When do we fear God above all things?**
We fear Him perfectly when we respect Him so highly that we do nothing against His will.

**5. When do we love God above all things?**
We love Him perfectly when we regard Him as our dearest friend and gladly do His will.

**6. When do we trust in God above all things?**
We trust Him above all things when we are sure that only He can and will take care of us.

**7. What do some people worship instead of the true God?**
Some people worship idols.

**8. What is an idol?**
An idol is any person or thing that receives the fear, love, and trust that belong to God.

**9. Why is it sinful to worship idols?**
God has forbidden idol worship.

**10. Why is it useless to worship idols?**
Idols are false gods who can neither hear nor help us.

**11. Name some idols that people worship?**
Many people worship idols made of wood and stone. Some people make food and drink most important in their lives, some make money and power most important in their lives, and some people spend their lives seeking pleasure and honor.

**12. When do we keep the First Commandment?**
We keep this commandment when serving God is our most important activity.

## WORD STUDY

*bondage:* slavery

*confidence:* trust

*idol:* a false god

*graven image:* carved statue; likeness; some people worship graven images

*worship:* the act of showing highest honor to God

## HYMN STANZA

Holy Father, holy Son,
Holy Spirit, three we name You,
Though in essence only one;
Undivided God we claim You
And, adoring, bend the knee
While we own the mystery.

*LW* 171:5

# PRAYER

Almighty and everlasting God, You enable me to move, think, and live. Give me, I pray, a strong faith in You so that I fear, love, and trust You in all that I do. I ask this through Jesus Christ, my Redeemer. Amen.

# WHAT THIS MEANS TO ME

Through the gracious work of the Holy Spirit, I always remember that the triune God is my best and dearest friend. I will always try to serve Him with a godly life and stay away from everything that is contrary to His holy will. I will pray only to Him for help and worship Him as the only true God. With His blessing, I will give Him my heart (Proverbs 23:26).

# UNIT 5

## The Second Commandment

### God's Name

*You shall not misuse the name of the Lord your God.*

*What does this mean?*
We should fear and love God so that we do not curse,
swear, use satanic arts, lie, or deceive by His name, but
call upon it in every trouble, pray, praise, and give thanks.

## BIBLE STORY

### *The Ten Lepers*                    Luke 17:11–19

"Jesus, Master, have mercy on us!" was the hoarse,
painful cry of 10 lepers. In Jesus' time lepers were not
allowed to be with other people at all because leprosy was
thought to be a highly contagious disease. Whenever
anyone came near them, they had to cover their faces and
cry, "Unclean! Unclean!" They were banned from towns.
They could not go to the temple or a synagogue. Their
sickness was like a living death. Is it any wonder that
when they saw Jesus coming, they cried to Him for help?

The 10 lepers had heard of the wonderful miracles Jesus had done, so they felt sure that He could heal them, even though all the doctors had said they could never get well again. So they turned to the Lord Jesus for help.

"Go," said Jesus, "show yourselves to the priests." The priests were the public health officers of that time.

The lepers went to see the priest. After examining them, the priest said, "There is nothing wrong with you."

"But we were lepers," they answered.

"You are lepers no longer," replied the priest. "You have been cured."

How happy they were! How could they ever forget that Jesus had made them well! Only one of them, a Samaritan, went back to Jesus, however. Falling down at Jesus' feet, the man used his now healthy voice to glorify God and thank Jesus for His help. Sadly Jesus asked, "Were not 10 cleansed? Where are the other nine? Only this one foreigner came back to give glory to God!" Turning to the thankful man, Jesus said, "Get up! Go your way. Your faith has made you whole."

## QUESTIONS FOR DISCUSSION

1. **Why did 10 lepers come to Jesus for help?**

2. **How did Jesus answer their prayer?**

3. **Compare and contrast the responses of the lepers to this miracle.**

4. **Why was Jesus concerned that only one foreigner came back?**

5. **How does this Bible story reinforce the teachings of the Second Commandment?**

# BIBLE READINGS

I am the LORD; that is My name! Isaiah 42:8

You are to give Him the name Jesus. Matthew 1:21

If anyone curses his God, he will be held responsible. Leviticus 24:15

Do not swear falsely by My name. Leviticus 19:12

They worship Me in vain; their teachings are but rules taught by men. Matthew 15:9

Not everyone who says to Me, "Lord, Lord," will enter the kingdom of heaven. Matthew 7:21

The LORD will not hold anyone guiltless who misuses His name. Exodus 20:7

Call upon Me in the day of trouble; I will deliver you, and you will honor Me. Psalm 50:15

Praise the LORD, O my soul; all my inmost being, praise His holy name. Psalm 103:1

How good it is to sing praises to our God. Psalm 147:1

# BIBLE TEACHINGS

God's names tell us who God is, what He is like, and what He has done for us. Because God's names tell us so much about God, His names are precious to us. We must not even think of using God's name in a sinful way and damaging His reputation. Just as my name is precious to me and I do not want others to misuse it, so God does not want His names misused either.

It is sinful to use God's names in cursing, joking, or false and careless swearing. People who teach falsely or lead a wicked life and use the name of God to cover up the wrong they are doing are taking the name of God in vain.

We should remember, however, that God does want us to use His name correctly. In fact, we should use it often in prayer. God wants us to think of His love, to tell Him of our needs, and to thank and praise Him in word and song.

# QUESTIONS AND ANSWERS

**1. What is God's name?**

God's name is every name by which God has made Himself known to us, such as God, Lord, Almighty, Jesus Christ, Holy Spirit, Immanuel, Redeemer, and Yahweh.

**2. When do we sin against God's name?**

We sin against His name when we misuse the name of the Lord our God.

**3. How might God's name be misused?**

God's name is misused when someone curses, swears, participates in satanic activities, lies, or uses His name to deceive others.

**4. What is cursing?**

Cursing is blaspheming God or calling on God to bring evil on others or ourselves.

**5. What is swearing?**

Swearing is calling on God to witness the truth of what we say and asking God to punish us if we do not tell the truth.

**6. When is swearing sinful? When is it proper to swear?**

Swearing is sinful when it is done falsely, carelessly, or needlessly. We may swear that we will tell the truth in a court of law.

**7. Why is using satanic arts sinful?**

In these activities God's name is used without His permission and promise. In many of these activities people try to use God's name and power to do things that are wicked and against His will.

**8. How do false prophets lie by God's name?**
When people preach or teach their own thoughts as if these were the Word of God, they are false prophets. Their teachings are lies. Only teachings that agree with God's Word should be taught to others. God's message of salvation through Jesus' suffering, death, and resurrection should be the focus of our teaching.

**9. How does a hypocrite use God's name in vain?**
A hypocrite misuses God's name by pretending to be Christian.

**10. How should we use God's name?**
We use God's name properly when we call on God for help in times of trouble, when we talk to God in prayer, when we thank Him for His blessings, and when we praise Him for being a great God.

**11. Why should we call upon God in every trouble?**
We should pray to God when we have troubles because He has promised to help us whenever we need it. He is always present to hear our prayers and has the power to answer them in a way that is best for us. Frequently God helps us through our troubles rather than removing them.

**12. For what should we praise God?**
Christians especially praise God for His wisdom, love, and mercy that He has given to us by giving His own Son to suffer, die, and rise from the dead so that our sins could be forgiven.

**13. When we remember God's goodness to us, what might Christians do in response?**
God's great love for people, shown through Jesus, moves Christians to thank Him with lives of joyful, obedient service and to offer Him many prayers and songs of praise. Since Christians have experienced God's love and care, they also tell others about what God has done for them.

# WORD STUDY

*to blaspheme:* to speak evil of God or sacred things

*to deceive:* to mislead

*hypocrite:* a person who pretends to be better than he or she is

*Samaritans:* people who believed the temple should be on Mount Gerizim rather than in Jerusalem; hatred existed between Jews and Samaritans because of this issue and others

*witchcraft:* magic power to do evil

*Yahweh:* God's proper, unique name in Hebrew, written with all capital letters in most English Bibles as LORD.

# HYMN STANZAS

How sweet the name of Jesus sounds
In a believer's ear!
It soothes our sorrows, heals our wounds,
And drives away all fear.

O Jesus, Shepherd, Guardian, Friend,
My Prophet, Priest, and King,
My Lord, my Life, my Way, my End,
Accept the praise I bring.

*LW* 279:1, 5

# PRAYER

Your name is holy, O Lord God of Hosts. Help me to keep Your name holy at all times. Prevent me from saying or doing anything that would dishonor Your name. Send Your Holy Spirit to me so that I honor You with my voice, my talents, and my thoughts every day of my life. Grant me this for the sake of Jesus Christ, my Lord, who is my Savior. Amen.

# WHAT THIS MEANS TO ME

Because God's names identify my God, who has loved and saved me, God's names are precious to me. By God's grace I will use them often to sing or speak prayers to Him, to thank Him for His gifts to me, and to praise Him for being a gracious God. I pray that I will never use His name thoughtlessly or for shameful cursing or swearing!

# UNIT 6

## The Third Commandment

### God's Word

*Remember the Sabbath day by keeping it holy.*

### What does this mean?

We should fear and love God so that we do not despise preaching and His Word, but hold it sacred and gladly hear and learn it.

# BIBLE STORY

### The Child Jesus in the Temple

Luke 2:41–52

When He was a boy, Jesus lived in Nazareth, a small town in Galilee. Each year His parents, Joseph and Mary, went to Jerusalem to take part in the Passover festival at the temple with Jews from all over the world. As was the custom, when Jesus was 12 years old, He was able to go along.

Traveling to the Passover festival was an exciting time. It was a time to visit with friends and relatives. Each step brought the people closer to Jerusalem, the city of God's people. Reaching the top of the last hill and see-

ing the city spread before them was a special thrill! In the distance was the beautiful temple of God.

Celebrating the Passover was both a solemn and a joyful time. Sacrifices were offered to remind the people of God's promise to send a Messiah, who would deliver them. A special meal reminded them of God's delivering the Israelites of long ago from Egypt.

After the festival Joseph and Mary left for home along with many of their friends from Nazareth. Jesus' parents thought He was somewhere in the crowd, traveling with the other children. In the evening of the first day on their way home, Mary and Joseph discovered that Jesus was not with the group! How worried they became! Back they rushed to Jerusalem, looking for Him everywhere. Finally, three days later, they found Him in the temple. He was sitting among the many wise teachers. He had surprised everyone with His understanding of God's Word. Mary cried, "Son, why have You done this? Your father and I were extremely worried. We looked for You everywhere."

"Why did you look for Me?" Jesus answered. "Didn't you know that I would be about My Father's business?" Jesus' parents didn't understand exactly what He meant.

Then He went back to Nazareth with Mary and Joseph. He was obedient to them. Mary remembered all these things and thought about them. Jesus grew physically as He matured in wisdom. In all that He did, He pleased both God and the people who knew Him.

## QUESTIONS FOR DISCUSSION

1. **Why did Joseph and Mary travel to Jerusalem each year?**

2. **How old was Jesus when He went along with them?**

3. **What did Jesus find so interesting in the temple?**

4. **How did Jesus show His love for the Word of God?**

5. **How may we show our love for the Word of God?**

## BIBLE READINGS

May the words of my mouth and the meditation of my heart be pleasing in Your sight, O LORD, my Rock and my Redeemer. Psalm 19:14

The Son of Man is Lord of the Sabbath. Matthew 12:8

Do not let anyone judge you . . . with regard to a religious festival . . . or a Sabbath day. Colossians 2:16

I love the house where You live, O LORD, the place where Your glory dwells. Psalm 26:8

He who belongs to God hears what God says. John 8:47

They devoted themselves to the apostles' teaching and to the fellowship, to the breaking of bread and to prayer. Acts 2:42

Let the Word of Christ dwell in you richly. Colossians 3:16

Blessed rather are those who hear the Word of God and obey it. Luke 11:28

These are the Scriptures that testify about Me. John 5:39

# BIBLE TEACHINGS

In Old Testament times the people of God were commanded to keep the Sabbath, the seventh day of the week. They kept the Sabbath by resting from all work and by hearing the Word of God.

Now, in New Testament times, we no longer need to follow those ceremonial laws. Yet God wants us to hear and study His holy Word regularly, to use the Sacraments, and to thank and praise Him for His love and care for us. In order to do this, Christians in most areas of the world worship regularly on Sunday. They celebrate Christmas, Easter, and Pentecost festivals and use the seasons of the church year to guide their spiritual life.

The Holy Spirit nurtures our faith when we regularly read and study the Bible. We honor His Word when we willingly support those who preach and teach it. God promises rich blessings when we study His Word faithfully and regularly participate in worship.

# QUESTIONS AND ANSWERS

**1. How did God's people in the Old Testament keep the Sabbath day holy?**

They rested from their daily work, worshiped, and heard the Word of God.

**2. Why are God's people in New Testament times not required to keep the seventh day as a Sabbath?**

Since Jesus, the promised Messiah, has come, the Old Testament ceremonial laws that looked forward to the Messiah no longer need to be followed. Jesus has ful-filled the Old Testament Sabbath requirement.

**3. Why do we worship on Sunday and celebrate the festivals of the church year?**

We worship on Sunday and celebrate the festivals of the church year so that we may receive God's grace and offer Him our thanks and praise. The church fes-tivals help us study the life and teachings of Jesus.

**4. Why did the first Christian church choose Sunday as the day of worship?**

Since Christ rose from the dead on a Sunday, they chose to worship on that day each week.

**5. When do we sin against the Third Command-ment?**

We sin against the Third Commandment when we neglect attending church and studying the Bible faith-fully.

**6. What may be some good reasons for not attend-ing church?**

When we do necessary work to ensure the safety of the community, when we do works of mercy, or when we are sick, we may not be able to worship with oth-ers. When this happens, we should attempt to find other times to worship with fellow believers. We should plan our time wisely so that family activities, sports, and other involvements do not interfere with faithful worship.

**7. When do we keep the Third Commandment?**

When we come into God's presence to receive His grace in Christ Jesus, and, on our part, offer ourselves to Him in grateful service, we are obeying the Third Commandment. Faithful church attendance, personal devotions, and Bible study are ways to keep the Third Commandment.

**8. How do we receive God's grace in Christ Jesus?**

We receive God's grace when we faithfully use God's Word, receive the Sacrament, and believe His promises.

**9. How do we offer ourselves to God in grateful service?**

We serve God when we faithfully do our daily work in ways that honor God. We also serve Him as we support the proclamation of the Gospel with our gifts of money and as we work on church committees or teach Bible class. Some serve God by becoming pastors, Christian teachers, or other full-time church workers.

**10. What should prompt us to support the church and to do good to all people?**

Christ's love for us creates love in our hearts. Our love for Christ, for His church, and for those who do not yet trust in Jesus prompts us to support the ministries of the church and to do good to others as we find opportunity.

**11. Why is it that people who profess love for Christ sometimes do not support His work?**

People have many reasons for not supporting the work of sharing the Gospel. Many place a higher priority on doing and purchasing things that they want than they place on supporting ministry. Some who profess love for Jesus do not realize that God wants them to share the Gospel with others and to support this work with their time and money.

12. **Why does the Bible say that people rob God when they do not adequately support the church?**
   When people do not support the sharing of the Gospel with their gifts, they withhold from God the time, talents, and treasure that He has a right to expect from His grateful, redeemed children.

13. **How should we use all that we are and all that we possess?**
   We should use all of our gifts from God to bring Him glory. Special gifts should regularly be given to support His work.

14. **Why should we use all our gifts for the glory of God?**
   God, through the sacrifice of His Son on the cross, has given to us the gift of eternal salvation. In response to His love for us, we try to use all His gifts to His glory. In addition, God is the real owner of everything; we are only stewards, or caretakers, of the gifts He has given to us.

15. **What promises does God give to those who love His Word and support His church?**
   Jesus said, "Blessed . . . are those who hear the Word of God and obey it" (Luke 11:28). He also told His disciples, "Give, and it will be given to you" (Luke 6:38).

# WORD STUDY

*habitation:* dwelling; home

*meditation:* quiet thought

*to redeem:* to buy back; to free mankind from sin, death, and the power of the devil

*Sabbath:* the Old Testament day of rest and worship

*Remember the Sabbath Day.*

# Hymn Stanza

Dearest Jesus, at Your Word
We have come again to hear You;
Let our thoughts and hearts be stirred
And in glowing faith be near You
As the promises here given
Draw us wholly up to heaven.

*LW* 202:1

# Prayer

Dear Lord Jesus, You said that those who hear Your Word and obey it would be blessed. Please send me Your Holy Spirit so that through my Bible reading at home and my Bible study at church and school I will receive Your blessings. Help me always use Your name to sing Your praises and to honor You everywhere I go. In Your name I ask this. Amen.

# What This Means to Me

Hearing and learning God's Word is as important to me as food is to my body. I know that failing to do this is sinning against God and damaging to my own faith. Therefore I will feed my soul by faithfully reading my Bible, by listening attentively when God's Word is read and taught in family devotions, and by gladly attending church. I pray that the Holy Spirit would help me trust God's Word so that I know the blessings of forgiveness through Jesus, my Savior.

# UNIT 7
## The Fourth Commandment

### God's Representatives

*Honor your father and your mother.*

*What does this mean?*
We should fear and love God so that we do not despise or anger our parents and other authorities, but honor them, serve and obey them, love and cherish them.

## BIBLE STORY

### *How Joseph Honored His Father*     Genesis 47:7–12

Joseph was a ruler of Egypt, second only to Pharaoh, the king. All the people of Egypt had been commanded to honor and serve him.

For many years Joseph's father, Jacob, had been a shepherd living in Canaan. When Jacob was very old, Joseph invited him to come to Egypt and live with him. When Jacob came, Joseph hurried to meet him. He put

his arms around his aged father and hugged him. He was so happy to have his father with him that he cried.

Even though Joseph was a great lord of Egypt and his father was a shepherd, Joseph gave his father all the honor and love that he could. He introduced his father to the king, who gave Joseph a valuable piece of land for his father's home.

As long as Jacob lived, Joseph did all that he could to give his father everything he needed and to keep him happy and contented. When Jacob died, Joseph buried him with great honor and mourned his death for many days.

## QUESTIONS FOR DISCUSSION

1. **What does it mean to honor someone?**

2. **How did Joseph honor his father?**

3. **Describe a variety of ways you can honor your parents.**

## BIBLE READINGS

Love your neighbor as yourself. Matthew 22:39

Children, obey your parents in everything. Colossians 3:20

"Honor your father and mother"—which is the first commandment with a promise. Ephesians 6:2

Rise in the presence of the aged, show respect for the elderly and revere your God. Leviticus 19:32

Everyone must submit himself to the governing authorities, for there is no authority except that which God has established. The authorities that exist have been established by God. Romans 13:1

We must obey God rather than men! Acts 5:29

# BIBLE TEACHINGS

As God planned for families, He intended that our parents be our best earthly friends. God has given parents the authority and responsibility to care for their children, to provide guidance as they grow, and to discipline (disciple) them for Christian living. Others to whom God has given authority over us are our teachers and the officials of our government.

It is a great sin against God when we disobey, despise, or in any way hurt our parents and others who have authority over us.

The Fourth Commandment says that God wants us to love our father and mother dearly, to thank Him for having given them to us, and to do all we can to honor and respect them.

God promises the special blessing of a long and happy life when we gladly do all that His representatives ask of us.

However, if they should ever tell us to do something against God and His Word, we must then obey God's Word.

# QUESTIONS AND ANSWERS

1. **What does God require of us in the Fourth Commandment?**
   In this commandment God says He wants us to honor those whom He has placed over us in our home, our church, our school, our place of work, and our government.

2. **Why must we honor our parents and others who have authority over us?**
   We honor our parents because God has appointed them to serve in His place, as His representatives, to care for us.

3. **When do we sin against these people who are God's representatives?**
   We sin against God's representatives when we despise them, refuse to obey them, or hurt them in any way.

4. **What might children do that would cause their parents to become angry?**
Children anger their parents when they disobey them or do evil things.

5. **What type of relationship does God want us to have with our parents?**
God wants parents and children to love each other dearly; honor and serve each other, as Jesus served us; and do all we can to ensure each other's happiness.

6. **Why should we honor our father and mother?**
It is God's will that we do this. God has given them the responsibility of caring for us.

7. **What other reasons do we have for honoring our parents?**
God gives us many blessings through our parents. By honoring them, we honor God and thank Him for His blessings.

8. **When especially do our parents need our love?**
Our parents especially need our love and care when they are sick, lonely, or unable to care for themselves.

9. **What does God promise to children who honor their parents?**
God promises that when you honor your parents it will "go well with you and that you may enjoy long life on the earth" (Ephesians 6:3).

10. **Is there ever a time when we must disobey our parents or others in authority?**
We may disobey them when they tell us to do something that is against God's will or His Word.

## WORD STUDY

*esteem:* high regard; thinking highly of someone
*to provoke:* to make angry
*representative:* one who has the right to act or speak for another
*subject:* obedient

# Hymn Stanzas

Jesus, Savior, wash away
All that has been wrong today;
Make me more like You each day
In all that I do and say.

Let my near and dear ones stand
In the hollow of Your hand;
Oh, bring me and all I love
To Your happy home above.

*LW* 503:2–3

# Prayer

Dear heavenly Father, bless my parents and all those whom You have placed over me. Help me so that I do not grieve or embitter them. Forgive me when I sin against them. By Your Spirit help me willingly honor, serve, love, cherish, and obey them. In Jesus' name I pray. Amen.

# What This Means to Me

God wants me to serve, obey, love, and honor my parents, teachers, government authorities, and all others whom He has placed over me. God does not want me to disobey, despise, or hurt my parents or other authorities in any way. Out of love for God, I will love them. When I do this, God promises that I will receive many blessings. When I fail, I know that God forgives me for Jesus' sake.

# UNIT 8

## The Fifth Commandment

God's Gift of Life

*You shall not murder.*

**What does this mean?**
We should fear and love God so that we do not hurt or harm our neighbor in his body, but help and support him in every physical need.

## BIBLE STORY

### *The Parable of the Good Samaritan*

Luke 10:25–37

The road from Jerusalem down to Jericho was steep and rough. It led through wild mountain country, where robbers could easily hide. One day a traveler walked down this road. Suddenly robbers attacked him, took all he had, beat him, and left him half dead.

After a while a priest came along the road. When he saw the poor wounded man, he quickly crossed to the other side of the road and hurried away. Soon, along came a Levite, a servant in God's temple. He also took one look at the suffering man and continued on his way.

Finally, a Samaritan came along. (Samaritans were Israel's enemies.) When he saw the bleeding stranger, he stopped at once. First he washed the man's wounds by pouring oil and wine on them. Then he bandaged them, lifted the man up on his donkey, and brought him to an inn. There he stayed up all night and took care of him.

The next day the Samaritan had to be on his way again. Before he left, he went to the innkeeper and said, "Here is some money. Take care of the man until he is well again. If this is not enough money, I will pay you the rest when I come again."

This is a story Jesus told when a man asked, "Who is my neighbor?"

## QUESTIONS FOR DISCUSSION

1. **What happened to the traveler? How are we like this traveler?**

2. **How did the priest and the Levite act toward him?**

3. **What did the Samaritan do when he saw the wounded man?**

4. **How does the Samaritan remind us of God? Why is the Samaritan a good illustration of how a person is to obey the Fifth Commandment?**

5. **By telling this parable, what was Jesus trying to teach the man and us?**

## BIBLE READINGS

Whoever sheds the blood of man, by man shall his blood be shed. Genesis 9:6

Anyone who hates his brother is a murderer, and

you know that no murderer has eternal life in him.
1 John 3:15

Out of the heart come evil thoughts, murder.
Matthew 15:19

If your enemy is hungry, feed him; if he is thirsty, give him something to drink. Romans 12:20

Blessed are the merciful, for they will be shown mercy. Matthew 5:7

Blessed are the peacemakers, for they will be called sons of God. Matthew 5:9

Love your enemies. Matthew 5:44

Be kind and compassionate to one another, forgiving each other, just as in Christ God forgave you. Ephesians 4:32

*Be kind to one another*

## BIBLE TEACHINGS

Our life is a very precious gift of God. Through the Fifth Commandment God protects human life.

In this commandment God forbids us to do or say anything by which our own or anyone else's life may be taken, shortened, endangered, or made unhappy. God considers hatred or even angry thoughts to be murder. Only the government has God's permission to punish someone by taking his or her life (capital punishment) or to order someone to fight in a just war. God forbids other forms of murder also, including suicide, abortion, and euthanasia (mercy killing).

In our daily lives God does not want us to try to get even with anyone or get revenge. Rather, we are to love all people, even our enemies, as did the Samaritan. We should do everything we can to prevent people from being harmed in any way. God wants us to be kind and forgiving toward others, as He has forgiven and loved us through His Son, Jesus. He wants us to help and befriend our neighbor in every possible way we can.

# QUESTIONS AND ANSWERS

1. **What does God forbid when He says, "You shall not murder"?**
   In this commandment God says that no one should kill anyone else. God also forbids us to physically hurt anyone or ourselves in body or in spirit.

2. **How is our neighbor hurt or harmed in her body?**
   Our neighbor is hurt by being injured or killed.

3. **How is our neighbor hurt in his spirit?**
   We hurt others in spirit when we make them angry or unhappy by saying or doing mean things to them.

4. **How do we commit murder in our heart?**
   We commit murder in our heart when we hate someone.

5. **What does the Bible say of the person who hates another?**
   The Bible says, "Anyone who hates his brother is a murderer" (1 John 3:15).

6. **When do we injure ourselves in our body?**
   We may injure ourselves in many ways, including eating improperly; abusing our body with drugs, alcohol, or tobacco; not getting proper rest or exercise; subjecting ourselves to unnecessary dangers; neglecting needed medical care; or by committing suicide.

7. **Why should we take good care of our body?**
   Our body is a sacred trust from the Lord; we are stewards of our bodies.

8. **Why is God the only one who has the right to end human life?**
   God created and gave life, and He alone has the right to end it.

9. **To whom has God given the right to take human life for the punishment of crime?**
   God has given this right to the government.

10. **How might we help and defend our neighbor?**
We should help him when he needs help, defend him when he is falsely accused, and seek to further his welfare at all times.

11. **Why is it not easy to help and befriend our enemies?**
Due to the sinful human nature that is ours since the fall into sin, we defend ourselves and hate those who wrong us. The evil they do to us easily moves us to hate them in return.

12. **What does God require from us in the Fifth Commandment?**
God asks us to love all people, even our enemies.

13. **How should we act toward those who have wronged us?**
We should be kind and forgiving to those who have wronged us. God has treated us kindly by forgiving our sins for Jesus' sake. He has done this even though we have wronged Him by our sin.

# WORD STUDY

*to injure:* to hurt or harm

*remorse:* deep sorrow for having done wrong

*revenge:* returning evil for evil

*steward:* one who manages another's property

*suicide:* killing oneself on purpose

# Hymn Stanza

In sickness, sorrow, want, or care,
Each other's burdens help us share;
May we, where help is needed, there
Give help as though to You.

*LW* 397:5

# Prayer

Loving Savior, take out of my heart all anger and hatred. Teach me to love others as You have loved me. Make me gentle and understanding, kind and forgiving, willing to help my neighbor at all times. Through Jesus Christ, my Lord, I pray. Amen.

# What This Means to Me

My neighbor's life and happiness are just as important to him as my life and happiness are to me. Through my Baptism the Holy Spirit empowers me to be kind and forgiving toward others, always keeping in mind the kindness and forgiveness that Jesus shows toward me. By God's grace I will guard against hatred, envy, quarreling, and any other actions that could hurt or harm others in any way.

# UNIT 9

## The Sixth Commandment

### God's Gift of Marriage

*You shall not commit adultery.*

*What does this mean?*
We should fear and love God so that we lead a sexually pure and decent life in what we say and do, and husband and wife love and honor each other.

## BIBLE STORY

### *How Joseph Kept Himself Pure*

Genesis 39:1–23

Poor Joseph! His brothers treated him cruelly. They hated him so much that they wanted to kill him. They got rid of him by selling him as a slave. He was taken to Egypt and sold to Potiphar, the captain of the king's guard.

Even then, the Lord was with Joseph and blessed him. Potiphar eventually thought so much of Joseph that he put him in charge of everything he owned. Everything might have been well had not Potiphar's wicked wife wanted him to

sleep with her. One day, when he went into the house to do some work, she tempted him again. Joseph told her, "How . . . could I do such a wicked thing and sin against God?" (Genesis 39:9). Then he pulled away from her, left the coat he was wearing in her grasp, and fled the house.

This reply made the woman very angry. When her husband came home, she accused Joseph of tempting her and showed the coat that Joseph had left as proof of her accusation. As a result, Potiphar had Joseph placed in jail. It seemed that Joseph's life had again taken a turn for the worse. He was a prisoner in the king's jail, alone and friendless in a strange land.

Even in jail, God was still with Joseph. God blessed him in many ways. He had honored God by living a pure life according to God's commands.

## QUESTIONS FOR DISCUSSION

**1. How did Joseph become a slave?**

**2. What did Potiphar's wife ask Joseph to do?**

**3. What was his answer?**

**4. How did God deal graciously with Joseph?**

## BIBLE READINGS

What God has joined together, let man not separate. Matthew 19:6

Husbands, love your wives, just as Christ loved the church and gave Himself up for her. Ephesians 5:25

Out of the heart come evil thoughts, murder, adultery, sexual immorality, theft, false testimony, slander. Matthew 15:19

It is shameful even to mention what the disobedient do in secret. Ephesians 5:12

Create in me a pure heart, O God. Psalm 51:10

Keep yourself pure. 1 Timothy 5:22

Flee the evil desires of youth, and pursue righteousness, faith, love and peace, along with those who call on the Lord out of a pure heart. 2 Timothy 2:22

My son, if sinners entice you, do not give in to them. Proverbs 1:10

## BIBLE TEACHINGS

The Sixth Commandment teaches me that husbands and wives may not break the union that God Himself makes when they promise to marry each other. Husbands and wives should be loving and faithful to each other as long as they live.

According to God's will, *all* people, married or unmarried, should be pure in heart, clean in speech, and decent in life.

Studying God's Word, praying, and working and engaging in wholesome activities will help us fight against unclean thoughts and actions. Remembering that we are Christ's through our Baptism will help us live pure lives.

## QUESTIONS AND ANSWERS

**1. What is marriage?**
Marriage is the lifelong union of a husband and wife.

**2. What does God require of married people?**
God wants married people to be faithful, loving, and helpful to each other as long as they live.

**3. What is adultery?**
A substance is adulterated when an impure substance is added to it. Those who have sexual relations with someone other than their spouse are guilty of adultery because they add an impurity to their marriage.

**4. What does God expect of all people, young and old, married and unmarried?**
God expects all people to live according to His Word by being pure in heart, clean in speech, and decent in their life.

**5. Why should we stay away from companions who consistently do not want to live according to God's Word?**
Companions who do not want to live according to God's Word may lead us into sin. Unfortunately, sometimes even our Christian friends lead us to sin. Remembering Jesus' love for us, especially as He gave His life on the cross for our forgiveness, is a powerful tool to help us help each other live godly lives.

**6. Why should we avoid impure things?**
Impure things, whether they are substances, thoughts, or activities, will hurt our bodies and souls. In thankfulness to God for His love for us, we who love Jesus seek to avoid adding impure things to our lives. Instead, God's Spirit helps us live lives of praise and thanksgiving to Him.

**7. Whom do we drive away by unclean thoughts, words, and deeds?**
We drive away God's Holy Spirit and the holy angels, who want to help us honor God in all that we do.

**8. Why are unclean activities often done in secret?**
Evildoers are ashamed of their unclean activities and hope to hide them from God and other people.

**9. Why is it foolish to think that an unclean activity can be hidden from God?**
God is omniscient; He knows all things.

**10. What purifies the human heart?**
The Word of God announcing that our sins are forgiven for Jesus' sake purifies the human heart.

**11. How does the Word of God purify our heart?**
God's Word of forgiveness cleanses our heart from all sin and implants love for Jesus in us. "The blood of Jesus, His Son, purifies us from all sin" (1 John 1:7).

**12. What prayer might we say to help stop having evil desires?**
We might pray the prayer of King David, "Create in me a pure heart, O God" (Psalm 51:10).

**13. What else can help us lead a pure and decent life in word and action?**
Working hard and faithfully at what we do, participating in clean and wholesome activities, and choosing companions who love Jesus can help us lead pure and decent lives that honor God.

## WORD STUDY

*adultery:* making something impure by adding impurities to it, such as having sex with someone who is not your marriage partner

*chaste:* clean; pure

*entice:* to tempt or lure into an activity or thought

*fornication:* having sex with someone to whom you are not married

*spouse:* husband or wife

*vanity:* false pride

*Create in me a clean heart, O Lord*

# Hymn Stanza

Your living Word shine in our heart
And to a new life win us.
With seed of light implant the start
Of Christlike deeds within us.
Help us uproot what is impure,
And while faith's fruits in us mature,
Prepare us for Your harvest.

*LW* 336:2

# Prayer

"Create in me a clean heart, O God, and renew a right spirit within me." May I always remember that my body is the temple of the Holy Spirit—that You live in me. Give me strength, Lord Jesus, to be pure in thoughts, words, and actions. O Father in heaven, make me pure within. Amen.

# What This Means to Me

The devil and sinners about me, as well as my own sinful nature, are constantly tempting me to think unclean thoughts, to say hurtful and suggestive things, and to do ungodly actions. Trusting God's Word, praying, and participating in wholesome activities are my best defenses against committing such evils. With God's help I can resist telling smutty stories, looking at indecent pictures, or doing impure things in secret. These words from Scripture can guide me: "Whatever is true, whatever is noble, whatever is right, whatever is pure, whatever is lovely, whatever is admirable—if anything is excellent or praiseworthy—think about such things" (Philippians 4:8).

# UNIT 10 — The Seventh Commandment

## God's Gift of Possessions

*You shall not steal.*

*What does this mean?*
We should fear and love God so that we do not take our neighbor's money or possessions, or get them in any dishonest way, but help him to improve and protect his possessions and income.

## BIBLE STORY

### *How Achan Was Punished for Stealing*                 Joshua 7:1–26

The imposing stone walls of Jericho had just fallen. Strong as they were, they could not stand up against the power of God. Now God told the people of Israel, "The people of Jericho are very wicked and ungodly. Destroy the city and burn everything in it. No one must take anything out of the city." The people did as God commanded.

Confidently they advanced against Ai, another nearby town in Canaan. "We will have no trouble taking Ai," their spies reported. "It is much smaller than Jericho, and God is fighting for us. We don't need our whole army to capture it."

How surprised they were when the people of Ai routed their army, chased it to the rocky bluffs, and destroyed it! What was wrong? Where was God's help? Sadly their leader Joshua asked God, "O Lord, why didn't You help us?"

God answered, "There is someone among you who did not obey My command to destroy everything in Jericho. He has stolen some things. I will not help you as long as that sin is not punished."

The guilty man turned out to be Achan. He had stolen a beautiful coat and some silver and gold and had hidden them in his tent. Achan and his family were stoned to death. When the guilty had been punished, God again helped His people against their enemies.

## QUESTIONS FOR DISCUSSION

1. **Why did God stop helping Israel?**

2. **Why was it wrong for Achan to take a few things found in Jericho?**

3. **How was Achan's sin discovered and punished (see Joshua 7)?**

## BIBLE READINGS

Do not use dishonest standards when measuring length, weight or quantity. Use honest scales and honest weights. Leviticus 19:35–36

Out of the heart come evil thoughts, murder, adultery, sexual immorality, theft, false testimony, slander. Matthew 15:19

The wicked borrow and do not repay, but the righteous give generously. Psalm 37:21

He who has been stealing must steal no longer, but

must work, doing something useful with his own hands, that he may have something to share with those in need. Ephesians 4:28

Do not forget to do good and to share with others, for with such sacrifices God is pleased. Hebrews 13:16

## BIBLE TEACHINGS

In the Seventh Commandment God protects our own and our neighbor's possessions. God says it is a sin to steal or to rob. In this commandment God also forbids every kind of dishonesty, such as weighing products dishonestly, overcharging for things that are sold, and cheating someone out of their possessions. It is also wrong to waste time at work or to borrow something and not return it in usable condition.

All these sins have their beginning in the selfish, loveless heart. To be sure, God forgives these sins because Jesus died on the cross to take the punishment for our sins and rose from the dead to enable us to serve Him (Luke 1:74).

The penitent sinner responds to God's love and forgiveness by loving others and gladly helping them keep their property and possessions, by protecting things they own from being harmed, and by helping them improve their situation. If someone needs something, we gladly share what we have with them.

# QUESTIONS AND ANSWERS

**1. What is the most open form of stealing?**
Robbery is the most obvious form of stealing. Taking something from someone else is only one way that this commandment is disobeyed.

**2. What are some other forms of stealing?**
Other forms of stealing include shortchanging someone when we sell something, shoplifting, cheating, overcharging, underpaying, not paying debts, and not doing an honest day's work in our occupation.

**3. What does God say about people who help others steal something or who knowingly use stolen things?**
God says, "The accomplice of a thief is his own enemy" (Proverbs 29:24). In other words, God does not want us to have anything to do with taking something that belongs to someone else.

**4. Why is damaging our neighbor's property a form of stealing?**
When something is damaged, its value and usefulness is reduced. When we damage someone else's toys or school materials, for example, that person will not be able to use them as planned. In effect, we have stolen that person's property.

**5. What should we do when we find something that is not ours?**
We should try to return it to its rightful owner.

**6. What should we do when our neighbor's property is in danger?**
We should do everything we can to protect it.

7. **How should we feel when God blesses our neighbor?**
   We should rejoice in the blessings God gives to our neighbor.

8. **What should we do when our neighbor needs help?**
   We should help our neighbor when we are able, even when it is not easy for us to do so.

9. **Why is protecting our neighbor's property and helping our neighbors keep their possessions a natural part of the Christian life?**
   By caring for the things that others own, the Christian is saying to God, "You have loved and cared for me by providing for me. You have done this especially when You sent Jesus to save me. To thank You, Lord, I help my neighbor take care of the blessings that You have given to her."

## Word Study

*unrighteousness:* wickedness

*usury:* charging too much interest

*possessions:* things that people own

# Hymn Stanza

Grant us hearts, dear Lord, to give You
Gladly, freely of Your own.
With the sunshine of Your goodness
Melt our thankless hearts of stone
Till our cold and selfish natures,
Warmed by You, at length believe
That more happy and more blessed
'Tis to give than to receive.

*LW* 402:2

# Prayer

Dear heavenly Father, take out of my heart every desire to steal or to be dishonest. Give me a loving heart to share what I have to help those who need it. Hear me, for Jesus' sake. Amen.

# What This Means to Me

All stealing is sin, including the stealing of small things. For Jesus' sake, I want to avoid dishonesty of any kind. I need to remember to return things that I borrow in good condition, to replace anything that I damage, and to be honest in every way.

# UNIT 11 — The Eighth Commandment

## God's Gift of a Good Reputation

*You shall not give false testimony against your neighbor.*

*What does this mean?*
We should fear and love God so that we do not tell lies about our neighbor, betray him, slander him, or hurt his reputation, but defend him, speak well of him, and explain everything in the kindest way.

## BIBLE STORY

### How Absalom Spoke Evil against His Father
2 Samuel 15:1–18:17

Absalom was one of King David's sons. He was very good-looking and was especially proud of his flowing, long hair. He had a selfish, wicked heart, however, and wanted to be king in place of his father. To achieve this goal, he worked to undermine his father's rule and reputation. Prince Absalom, for example, would stand near the palace gate. When people came to have King David

settle some of their lawsuits, Absalom would tell them, "If I were the judge in the land, everyone could come to me to settle things. I would give you a better deal than my father does."

This made many people think David was not treating them fairly and that it might be better if Absalom were king. By doing this Absalom stole the hearts of the people from his father, David. Absalom's words destroyed David's reputation.

When Absalom thought he had enough people on his side, he began to raise an army to fight against his father. When David had to leave Jerusalem, Absalom took advantage of this opportunity to declare himself king.

He didn't stay king very long. God was angry with him because of his sin. David's faithful soldiers defeated the rebels in a bloody battle. Absalom raced away from the battle on his mule. As he rode through the woods, his head got caught in the branches of a big oak tree. When his mule ran out from under him, he was left hanging from the tree branch. Against David's command to deal kindly with Absalom, one of David's generals, Joab, plunged javelins into Absalom as he hung there, killing him.

# QUESTIONS FOR DISCUSSION

1. **How did Absalom damage his father's reputation?**

2. **How was Absalom punished for his sin?**

3. **Describe what Absalom could have done to improve his father's reputation.**

## BIBLE READINGS

Each of you must put off falsehood and speak truthfully to his neighbor. Ephesians 4:25

A false witness will not go unpunished, and he who pours out lies will not go free. Proverbs 19:5

Brothers, do not slander one another. James 4:11

A gossip betrays a confidence, but a trustworthy man keeps a secret. Proverbs 11:13

Out of the heart come evil thoughts, murder, adultery, sexual immorality, theft, false testimony, slander. Matthew 15:19

"Do not plot evil against your neighbor, and do not love to swear falsely. I hate all this," declares the LORD. Zechariah 8:17

Speak up for those who cannot speak for themselves. . . . Defend the rights of the poor and needy. Proverbs 31:8–9

Love each other deeply, because love covers over a multitude of sins. 1 Peter 4:8

## BIBLE TEACHINGS

In the Eighth Commandment God protects our own and our neighbor's good name or reputation. Having a good name is worth much more than being rich.

We sin against the Eighth Commandment when we do or say anything that hurts someone's reputation. We damage people's reputations when we lie about them, give away their secrets, say evil things about them, or remain silent when others say evil things about them.

Love for God and our neighbors will make us defend our neighbors against lies, speak good things about them, and think of them as God's creation.

# Questions and Answers

**1. What has God done to protect our neighbor's good name and reputation?**

In this commandment God forbids us to do or to say anything that will hurt our neighbor's reputation.

**2. Why should we guard against even thinking something bad about our neighbor?**

Thinking evil about anyone is sinful and may lead to saying something that is false or doing something hurtful to that person.

**3. How may our neighbor's reputation be hurt or destroyed?**

Our neighbor's reputation will be hurt when we lie or say evil things about our neighbor, or when we keep silent when others slander him or her.

**4. What will a liar surely receive from God?**

An unrepentant liar will receive punishment from God, for God hates all lies.

**5. What should we do to protect our neighbor's good name?**

We should defend our neighbor against lies. We should also say good things about our neighbor whenever we can. When we hear something that we don't know about, we should put the best construction on the situation.

**6. When does our neighbor especially need protection against evil gossip and other forms of false witness?**

Our neighbor needs our help especially when absent and unabl to defend himself or herself.

7. **How do we put the best construction on our neighbor's words and deeds?**

We put the best construction on a situation when we truthfully explain the situation. God does not want us to lie to protect our neighbor.

8. **What will empower us to obey God's will in this matter?**

God's love for us in creating and redeeming us through Jesus, our Savior, will enable us, by God's grace, to protect our neighbor's reputation.

## Word Study

*charity:* Christian love and good will

*multitude:* a great number

*to offend:* to violate a law; to cause an injury to someone

*reputation:* good name; what others think of us

*to slander:* saying something false that damages someone's reputation

# Hymn Stanza

Keep me from saying words
That later need recalling;
Guard me lest idle speech
May from my lips be falling;
But when within my place
I must and ought to speak,
Then to my words give grace
Lest I offend the weak.

*LW* 371:3

# Prayer

O Lord, You are a God of truth and holiness. Pour the love of Christ into my heart so that I may always say things that are true and helpful. Help me to guard my tongue so that I do not say false or unkind words. Grant this, dear Father, for my Savior's sake. Amen.

# What This Means to Me

God's love for me given through Jesus, my Savior, calls me to do everything in my power to protect and preserve my neighbor's good name. For this reason I, by God's grace, will defend others when they are victims of lies and gossip, which would only injure their reputation. No lie is too small to be a sin in God's sight. I will remember that all lies are of the devil, for he is the father of lies. I will speak well of my neighbor whenever possible.

# UNIT 12

## The Ninth and Tenth Commandments

### God's Gift of Contentment

*You shall not covet your neighbor's house.*

**What does this mean?**
We should fear and love God so that we do not scheme to get our neighbor's inheritance or house, or get it in a way which only appears right, but help and be of service to him in keeping it.

*You shall not covet your neighbor's wife, or his manservant or maidservant, his ox or donkey, or anything that belongs to your neighbor.*

**What does this mean?**
We should fear and love God so that we do not entice or force away our neighbor's wife, workers, or animals, or turn them against him, but urge them to stay and do their duty.

## BIBLE STORY

### *How Ahab Got Naboth's Vineyard*  1 Kings 21:1–16

In addition to his palace, King Ahab of Israel had a beautiful summer home in Jezreel. He was very proud of this fine place and tried to improve it when he could.

Next to the king's estate was a vineyard that belonged to Naboth. Naboth treasured his vineyard because he had inherited it from his father.

One day King Ahab became very angry. He went to bed, turned his face toward the wall, and would not eat. When his wife, Jezebel, asked him what was wrong, he said, "Naboth has a vineyard next to my property that I want to make into a garden. I offered to pay him for it or to give him another vineyard, but he won't let me have it." In refusing the offer, Naboth had remembered God's command not to sell the inheritance of his father.

Jezebel said, "Aren't you the king in Israel? Can't you take what you want? Cheer up! I will get Naboth's vineyard for you."

The wicked queen then wrote a letter to the officials in Jezreel. "Call the people together for a big gathering," the letter said. "Put Naboth on trial in front of everyone. Have two scoundrels that you find somewhere say 'Naboth has cursed God and the king!' Then carry him away, and stone him to death."

The officials followed Jezebel's orders. When she heard the news that Naboth was dead, she hurried to King Ahab and told him, "Naboth is dead. Go and take your vineyard."

# QUESTIONS FOR DISCUSSION

**1. Why was Ahab angry?**

**2. Why wouldn't Naboth sell his vineyard?**

**3. Which of the two men was content with what he had?**

**4. How did Jezebel help Ahab get the vineyard?**

# BIBLE READINGS

The Lord looks at the heart. 1 Samuel 16:7

The love of money is a root of all kinds of evil. 1 Timothy 6:10

Out of the heart come evil thoughts, murder, adultery, sexual immorality, theft, false testimony, slander. Matthew 15:19

I would not have known what coveting really was if the law had not said, "Do not covet." Romans 7:7

Be content with what you have. Hebrews 13:5

Be holy because I, the Lord your God, am holy. Leviticus 19:2

# BIBLE TEACHINGS

Both the Ninth and the Tenth Commandments say, "You shall not covet." These commandments teach that we should not envy or try to get what our neighbor owns in a sinful way (coveting). Envy and coveting, sins in the sight of God, may lead to lying, stealing, adultery, and even murder if not controlled.

God wants our hearts filled with holy desires, thankful for our salvation in Jesus. He wants us to be content with what we have and to rejoice with our neighbor over the blessings He has given.

## QUESTIONS AND ANSWERS

**1. Why do people covet what belongs to others?**
People covet because of discontent, envy, greed, love of power, and other evil thoughts and desires that originate in the heart.

**2. What does God think of these evil thoughts and desires?**
According to God's Word, all evil thoughts and desires and covetous words and deeds are sinful.

**3. What may such evil desires lead to if they are not checked?**
Evil desires may lead to sinful deeds, such as complaining about God, stinginess, dishonesty, cruel treatment of others, stealing, adultery, murder, and war.

**4. Why must all people, even Christians, carefully watch their hearts?**
All people have evil thoughts and desires in their hearts. The devil tempts everyone.

**5. What is the will of God concerning our heart?**
God wants our heart to be filled with holy desires only.

**6. How do people sometimes seek to get their neighbor's property craftily?**
Dishonest people may try to get other people's property by tricking them, deceiving them, advertising something falsely, not providing full details about a contract, and by other deceitful means.

**7. How do people sometimes seek to get their neighbor's property by a show of right?**
These people make it appear as if they are helping their neighbor when, in actuality, they are cheating their neighbor out of his or her property.

**8. Why does a covetous person always desire more and more?**

A covetous person thinks that having more possessions will bring happiness, power, and security.

**9. How does God want us to feel about the things He gives to us?**

God wants us to be content with His blessings and to be willing to share them with those in need.

**10. How does God want us to feel toward our neighbor's property?**

God wants us to be happy when our neighbor prospers. He also wants us to do all we can to help our neighbor keep his or her property.

# WORD STUDY

*to covet:* to wish to have something that belongs to someone else

*craftily:* to act in an underhanded and cunning manner

*inheritance:* property or money received through a will from someone else

*to envy:* to be discontented at another person's good fortune and to harbor a desire to have the same good fortune

*to entice:* to coax away by offering an attractive inducement

*to estrange:* to encourage unfriendly thoughts and behavior where previously there had been friendliness

# HYMN STANZAS

"Come, follow Me," said Christ, the Lord,
"All in My way abiding;
Your selfishness throw overboard,
Obey My call and guiding.
Oh, bear your crosses, and confide
In My example as your guide."

"I teach you how to shun and flee
What harms your soul's salvation;
Your heart from ev'ry guile to free,
From sin and its temptation.
I am the Refuge of the soul
And lead you to your heav'nly goal."

*LW* 379:1, 4

# PRAYER

Almighty God, to whom all hearts are open, let Your Holy Spirit cleanse my secret thoughts. Help me avoid every evil thought and wish; preserve me from envy and covetousness. Enable me to rejoice in the prosperity of others, and grant me grace to be content with the things I have. Through Jesus Christ, my Lord, I pray. Amen.

## WHAT THIS MEANS TO ME

It is sinful to be envious of others and to covet things that other people have. By God's grace I will be satisfied with what He gives me and not be envious of things that others have. Since I have food and clothing, as the Scripture says, and as the Holy Spirit gives me strength, I will be content with that (1 Timothy 6:8).

# UNIT 13 The Close of the Commandments

## The Judgments and Promises of God

*What does God say about all these commandments?*
He says: "I, the Lord your God, am a jealous God, punishing the children for the sin of the fathers to the third and fourth generation of those who hate Me, but showing love to a thousand generations of those who love Me and keep My commandments." **[Ex. 20:5–6]**

*What does this mean?*
God threatens to punish all who break these commandments. Therefore, we should fear His wrath and not do anything against them. But He promises grace and every blessing to all who keep these commandments. Therefore, we should also love and trust in Him and gladly do what He commands.

## BIBLE STORY

### *The Fall into Sin*                    Genesis 3:1–24

When they lived in the Garden of Eden, Adam and Eve were perfectly happy. God had done everything to make them enjoy every moment of their lives. He had created them pure and holy. He had built a beautiful park, or paradise, to be their home. God came and talked with them. They could have enjoyed His company at all times. What more could they want?

God asked only one thing of them. "You are free to eat of any tree in the garden," He said, "but you must not eat from the tree of the knowledge of good and evil, for when you eat of it you will surely die," (Genesis 2:16).

One day Satan, the leader of the evil angels, set out to take all happiness away from Adam and Eve. He came into the garden in the form of a serpent and said to Eve, "Did God really say, 'You must not eat from this tree in the garden'? You will not die," the devil continued, "God simply does not want you to be as wise as He is."

Eve listened to the devil and ate some fruit from the forbidden tree. Then she gave some to Adam, and he ate it. Hardly had they tasted the fruit when they realized the devil had led them to do the one thing God had told them not to do. They were ashamed and afraid of God.

The Lord God soon came walking in the garden. Adam and Eve hid from Him. "Where are you?" God called. After trying to blame each other and the devil for what they had done, they confessed that they had eaten from the tree of which God had spoken. Then God condemned the devil and promised that a Savior would come who would crush the devil's power (Genesis 3:15).

God, as punishment for their sin, drove Adam and Eve out of the Garden of Eden. From that day on they had much suffering and sorrow because of their sin. Finally they would have to physically die, as God had said they would.

# QUESTIONS FOR DISCUSSION

1. **Describe what God had done to provide for Adam and Eve.**

2. **What had God told them not to do?**

3. **Why did they disobey God's command?**

4. **How were they punished for their sin?**

5. **After Adam and Eve sinned, how did God show His great love for them?**

# BIBLE READINGS

The LORD . . . said in His heart: "Never again will I curse the ground because of man, even though every inclination of his heart is evil from childhood."
Genesis 8:21

The soul who sins is the one who will die.
Ezekiel 18:20

The wages of sin is death. Romans 6:23

Sin entered the world through one man, and death through sin, and in this way death came to all men, because all sinned. Romans 5:12

I will put enmity between you and the woman, and between your offspring and hers; He will crush your head, and you will strike His heel. Genesis 3:15

Godliness has value for all things, holding promise for both the present life and the life to come.
1 Timothy 4:8

Do not be deceived: God cannot be mocked.
Galatians 6:7

# BIBLE TEACHINGS

God gave His commandments to all people. He wants everyone to obey His commandments. He is a jealous God; that is, He wants every commandment kept perfectly in thought, word, and deed.

God hates every sin, including sinful thoughts. If the sinner does not repent, God will punish him or her with eternal death. Such punishment is fully deserved because every sin is something done against God's holy will. This truth should make us afraid of God's anger and careful not to do anything against His commandments.

On the other hand, God promises to bless all those who love Him and keep His commandments. He showed His love to all people when He promised a Savior already to Adam and Eve immediately after they sinned. Even their offspring could have their sin forgiven through the promised Savior. This truth moves people to honor God by willingly obeying Him.

# QUESTIONS AND ANSWERS

1. **What does God say of Himself in the conclusion of the commandments?**
   He says, "I, the Lord your God, am a jealous God."

2. **Why does God call Himself a jealous God?**
   God wants us to love and obey Him only. God rightly expects that all honor and thanks be given to Him.

3. **Why does God have the right to expect obedience?**
   He is the creator of all things. He is the Lord of all and the rightful lawgiver.

4. **How does God want His commandments to be kept?**
   God wants His commandments to be kept perfectly in thought, word, and deed.

5. **What is sin?**
   Sin is every thought, desire, word, and deed that is contrary to God's Law. It is our inherited condition since the fall into sin.

6. **From whom have all people inherited their sinful condition?**
   All children have inherited sin from Adam and Eve through their ancestors.

7. **How does each person add to the sin of Adam?**
   Each day every person commits sinful acts.

8. **How does God show His anger toward those who sin?**
   God punishes them. He did this when Jesus was crucified on the cross.

9. **How severely does He punish them?**
   In His Word God says that children still experience the consequences of the sins of their ancestors.

10. **What should God's great anger over sin move us to do?**
    We should fear His wrath and not act contrary to His commandments.

11. **What does God show to those who love Him and keep His commandments?**
    God shows mercy to thousands of people who love Him and keep His commandments. In His mercy God sent Jesus to live, suffer, die, and rise for the sins of all people.

12. **God blesses obedience. What should this move us to do?**
    We should be moved to love God, trust Him, and willingly obey His commandments.

# WORD STUDY

*to assail:* to attack; the devil assails us

*to bruise:* to hurt; to crush

*enmity:* ill will; hatred; there will always be ill will between the devil and people

*generation:* people born in the same period of time

*grace:* God's undeserved mercy and kindness

*inclination:* the likely way for a person to be or act

*jealous:* requiring complete obedience

# HYMN STANZA

Lord Jesus, since You love me,
Now spread Your wings above me
And shield me from alarm.
Though Satan would devour me,
Let angel guards sing o'er me:
This child of God shall meet no harm.

*LW* 485:4

## PRAYER

I confess to You, God Almighty,
Father, Son, and Holy Spirit, that
I have sinned in thoughts,
words, and actions, through
my fault, my own fault.
Therefore I pray,
almighty God, have
mercy on me, forgive
all my sins, and
make my heart
clean within me.
Almighty and merciful
Lord, grant me pardon
and forgiveness for all
my sins, work true repen-
tance in me, and help
me change my sinful
ways. Give to me the
grace and comfort of the
Holy Spirit. Amen.

## WHAT THIS MEANS TO ME

God expects me to obey all His commandments.
He knows all my sins, and He holds me accountable for
every single sin, including my sinful thoughts. Unless I
repent of my sins and beg His forgiveness, He will punish me with eternal death. I know I must avoid making
Him angry by disobeying His will. Since I know I cannot even begin to keep track of all my sins, I entrust
myself to Him and His loving mercy, confident that He
has forgiven my sins because Jesus lived a perfect life
for me, was punished for my sins, died in my place, and
now is risen from the dead. Out of love for Him I will
attempt to gladly keep His commandments, through
the power of the Holy Spirit. I know that He will surely
bless me according to His will.

# UNIT 14

## The Close of the Commandments

### The Purposes and Fulfillment of the Law

## BIBLE STORY

### *The Rich Young Ruler*       Mark 10:17–22

One day a rich young man came running to Jesus. "Good Master," he asked, "what good thing must I do so that I may have eternal life?"

"You know the commandments," Jesus answered. "Keep them, and you will go to heaven."

"Which commandments?" the young man asked.

"Do not commit adultery; do not kill; do not steal; do not lie or bear false witness; honor your father and your mother; love your neighbor as yourself," Jesus told him.

"Oh," cried the young man, "I have kept all of those since I was a child! What else do I need to do?"

Jesus looked at him lovingly and answered, "The one thing you need to do yet is to sell all your property, give the money to the poor, and follow Me. Then you will have treasure in heaven."

The young man heard what Jesus told him. He had nothing to say. He loved his property and money more than anything else he had. He sadly walked away.

## QUESTIONS FOR DISCUSSION

1. **How did the rich young man hope to obtain eternal life?**

2. **What wrong opinion did he have of himself?**

3. **Why did Jesus ask the young man to sell his property?**

4. **What is the only way to heaven?**

## BIBLE READINGS

The Law is holy, and the commandment is holy, righteous and good. Romans 7:12

Law is made not for the righteous but for lawbreakers and rebels. 1 Timothy 1:9

A bad tree bears bad fruit. Matthew 7:17

Through the Law we become conscious of sin. Romans 3:20

I know that nothing good lives in me, that is, in my sinful nature. Romans 7:18

How can a young man keep his way pure? By living according to Your Word. Psalm 119:9

Christ redeemed us from the curse of the Law by becoming a curse for us. Galatians 3:13

## BIBLE TEACHINGS

The Law is holy and good because it comes from God. The Law, however, cannot make us holy or lead us to heaven. We cannot keep the Law (the Commandments) as God wants us to keep them. To keep the Law, we must love God perfectly with all our heart. All people are sinful, however. No one can love God perfectly.

Yet the Law of God serves very necessary and useful purposes. First, acting as a curb, it prevents many wicked deeds. Second, the Law acts like a mirror. It shows us how we look in the sight of God—evil in thought, word, and deed. It shows us that we are lost and condemned and that we cannot save ourselves. The Law shows us our need for a Savior. Finally, the Law serves as a ruler, showing us how God wants us to live in obedience to His commands.

Our Savior, Jesus Christ, has redeemed us from all our sins against the Law of God and from its curse.

## QUESTIONS AND ANSWERS

**1. Now that you have studied the Ten Commandments, what must you confess?**
I must confess that I have sinned against God's commandments in my thoughts, words, and deeds.

**2. What do you deserve because of your transgressions?**
I deserve God's wrath and punishment.

**3. Do you have any hope at all of being saved, since you have committed so many transgressions?**
Christ redeemed me from the curse of the Law by becoming a curse for us (Galatians 3:13).

**4. Where do you learn that you are freed from the curse of the Law?**
I learn this from the Gospel.

**5. What is the Gospel?**
The Gospel is the good news that Jesus kept the Law for me and died for my sins.

6. **Why will you always need strength from God to walk in the way of the Lord?**
Since "I know that nothing good lives in me, that is, in my sinful nature" (Romans 7:18), I will always need the power of the Holy Spirit to help me resist temptations.

7. **How can you hope to keep the commandments better in the future than you have in the past?**
I know that "it is God who works in [me] to will and to act according to His good purpose" (Philippians 2:13).

8. **Where in the catechism do you learn the Gospel?**
I learn the Gospel in the Second Chief Part of the catechism, the Apostles' Creed.

9. **Of what value has the study of the First Chief Part been to you?**
So far I have learned that the Law serves as a curb, a mirror, and a rule.

10. **In what way does the Law serve as a curb?**
The Law helps to stop the coarse outbursts of sin, like a curb helps keep a car on the road.

11. **In what way does the Law serve as a mirror?**
God's Law shows me what sin is: "Through the Law we become conscious of sin" (Romans 3:20).

12. **How does the Law serve as a ruler?**
The Law guides the Christian to live a life that pleases God, as a ruler guides a pencil to make a straight line.

13. **Who is the way to life everlasting?**
The Lord Jesus Christ is the way, the truth, and the life.

14. **Where in the catechism do we learn of this way?**
We learn of Jesus and His love for us in the creeds, such as the Apostles' Creed. A creed is a statement of what a person believes, teaches, confesses, and lives by.

# WORD STUDY

*corrupt:* rotten; wicked

*lawless:* paying no attention to the law

*precepts:* commandments; rules

*to prevent:* to keep from happening

*to redeem:* to buy back; to make free

*transgression:* breaking of the law; sin

## Christ is the Only Way

# HYMN STANZA

May we Your precepts, Lord, fulfill
And do on earth our Father's will
As angels do above;
Still walk in Christ, the living Way,
With all Your children and obey
The law of Christian love.

*LW* 389:1

# PRAYER

O holy and righteous God, Your Law shows me my sinful and lost condition. Have mercy on me. Forgive all my sins for Jesus' sake. Create in me a thankful heart so that I love and serve You with all my strength and do those things that are pleasing to You. I ask this through Jesus Christ, my Savior. Amen.

# WHAT THIS MEANS TO ME

God's Law, the Ten Commandments, is my only trustworthy guide to God-pleasing living. I must learn it, study it, and keep it in mind all the time so that I can faithfully walk in God's path. Since I can never keep

God's Law perfectly, I am thankful that Jesus kept the Law perfectly for me; by His suffering, death, and resurrection, He earned forgiveness from God for all my sins.

**Jesus kept the Law.**

# UNIT 15    The First Article—Creation

## God, the Creator

*"The earth is the Lord's, and everything in it."* (Psalm 24:1)

I believe in God, the Father Almighty, Maker of heaven and earth.

*What does this mean?*

I believe that God has made me and all creatures; that He has given me my body and soul, eyes, ears, and all my members, my reason and all my senses, and still takes care of them.

He also gives me clothing and shoes, food and drink, house and home, wife and children, land, animals, and all I have. He richly and daily provides me with all that I need to support this body and life.

He defends me against all danger and guards and protects me from all evil.

All this He does only out of fatherly, divine goodness and mercy, without any merit or worthiness in me. For all this it is my duty to thank and praise, serve and obey Him.

This is most certainly true.

# BIBLE STORY

### *How God Made All Things*          Genesis 1

"In the beginning God created the heavens and the earth."

First, God made light and divided the light from the darkness. He called the light day and the darkness night.

First Day

Second Day

Third Day

Fou

Evening and morning marked the first day in the history of the world.

During the next five days God created many new things. On the second day He separated the water in the sky from the water on earth and placed the heavens between them. On the third day God made the oceans, lakes, and rivers and commanded the dry land to appear. Then He covered the earth with grasses, shrubs, flowers, shade trees, and fruit trees of all kinds. The next day God placed brilliant lights in the sky that we call the sun, the moon, the planets, and the stars.

On the fifth day God made the many varieties of creatures that live in the water and in the air. Fish, whales, and birds of all sizes and colors appeared in abundance.

The sixth day was the greatest of all. In it God made all the different kinds of animals that live on land, including those that creep, those that jump, and those that run. Last and best of all, God made the first people, a man and woman.

When He was finished, God looked at everything He had made and saw that it was very good. God's work of creation was finished. On the seventh day God rested.

**Fifth Day**     **Sixth Day**     **Seventh Day**

# QUESTIONS FOR DISCUSSION

**1. How did the world begin to exist?**

**2. Tell what God made during the first six days of the world.**

**3. Which was the last and best of God's visible creatures?**

# BIBLE READINGS

In the beginning God created the heavens and the earth. Genesis 1:1

By Him all things were created: things in heaven and on earth, visible and invisible. Colossians 1:16

By the word of the LORD were the heavens made. Psalm 33:6

By faith we understand that the universe was formed at God's command. Hebrews 11:3

My help comes from the LORD, the Maker of heaven and earth. Psalm 121:2

I trust in You, O LORD; I say, "You are my God." Psalm 31:14

# BIBLE TEACHINGS

In the Bible we learn about many works of God.

The first work of God mentioned in the Bible is the creation of the world. In the beginning God, by His almighty Word, made all things. This same great and mighty God is my loving Father through Christ, my Savior. By His grace I trust Him for everything.

# QUESTIONS AND ANSWERS

**1. Which part of the catechism tells us about the work of the triune God?**
The Apostles' Creed tells us what God has done.

**2. What is a creed?**
A creed is a brief summary of what someone believes.

3. **Why is the oldest Christian creed called the Apostles' Creed?**
This creed summarizes the main teachings of the apostles.

4. **What are the main teachings of the apostles?**
The Apostles' Creed outlines these teachings by stating that God the Father created the universe, God the Son redeemed all people, and God the Holy Spirit creates faith and makes our faith grow.

5. **In what way is the Apostles' Creed a picture of the Holy Trinity?**
There is one creed but three articles, just as there is one God but three persons.

6. **Why do you call the First Person of the blessed Trinity the Father?**
The First Person in the Trinity is the Father of Jesus Christ and the Maker and Preserver of all things.

7. **How did God make heaven and earth?**
God made heaven and earth by using the power of His Word.

8. **How is this possible?**
"Our God is in heaven; He does whatever pleases Him" (Psalm 115:3).

9. **Why can our God do whatever pleases Him?**
God is almighty. He created everything by His powerful Word.

10. **Why do we believe this?**
God has said so, and we trust His Word.

11. **What two kinds of creatures has God made?**
God made visible and invisible creatures.

12. **Because of creation, to whom do you belong?**
Since God created life, I belong to God. We are God's workmanship, created in Christ Jesus to do good works (Ephesians 2:10).

**13. Why is it a privilege to live and serve your Creator?**

God, who created all things, is my Father also through Christ, my Savior. God not only gave me life, but He saved me and continues to care for me.

*"In the beginning God."*

## Word Study

*adoration:* worship

*creature:* something God has made

*invisible:* not able to be seen

*to preserve:* to uphold; to protect

*privilege:* favor; honor

*throng:* large number

*visible:* able to be seen

## Hymn Stanza

Praise to the Lord, the Almighty,
  the King of creation!
O my soul, praise Him,
  for He is your health and salvation!
Let all who hear
Now to His temple draw near,
  Joining in glad adoration!

*LW* 444:1

## Prayer

O almighty, everlasting God, Creator of heaven and earth, help me trust in You more and more. Move me to praise You for Your power, wisdom, goodness, and truth. Help me to believe that You are my loving Father through the work of Christ and that I am Your child. Each day increase my trust in You and Your dear Son, my Savior. Amen.

# WHAT THIS MEANS TO ME

Whenever I look at the grandeur of the majestic mountains, the rolling ocean, or the blue sky, I am reminded that the great and mighty God, my heavenly Father, created the heavens and the earth for my good. He wants me to use these blessings to His glory and for my own and my neighbor's good. I pray that I will always hope in God, who richly provides me with everything for my enjoyment (1 Timothy 6:17).

# UNIT 16     The First Article—Creation

Angels

*"Praise Him, all His angels." (Psalm 148:2)*

## BIBLE STORY

### How an Angel Protected the Three Men in the Fiery Furnace    Daniel 3:1–28

Mighty King Nebuchadnezzar of Babylon had fought against the kingdom of Judah and defeated it. He took many of the people of Judah with him back to Babylon as prisoners. They now had to live in a strange land.

Among the prisoners were three friends whose names were Shadrach, Meshach, and Abednego. They were godly young men who faithfully worshiped the true

God, even though they lived among the unbelieving people of Babylon.

King Nebuchadnezzar had a 90-foot-high golden image, or statue, placed in Babylon. At its dedication he proclaimed, "All people, no matter what language you speak, fall down and worship this statue whenever you hear the music of the horns and flutes. Anyone who doesn't worship this image will be thrown into a blazing furnace." Fearing for their lives, most people obeyed the king.

The three friends from Judah, however, refused to fall down and worship the statue. "We are not afraid of your fiery furnace," they told the king. "Our God, whom we serve, can deliver us from the blazing fire and rescue us from you. Even if He chooses not to, we will not worship your golden image."

The king became furious. After ordering that the furnace be made seven times hotter than usual, he ordered them thrown into the furnace.

Soon Nebuchadnezzar, who was watching the fire, cried out, "What is this? Didn't we put three men in the fire? I see four men walking around in the flames. The fourth looks like the Son of God." Quickly he called to the men to come out of the furnace. The fire had not touched them. Not even the smell of smoke was on their clothes.

Seeing what had happened, Nebuchadnezzar said, "Praise be to the God of Shadrach, Meshach, and Abednego, who has sent His angel and rescued His servants. They trusted in Him."

# Questions for Discussion

1. What did King Nebuchadnezzar order all the people to do?
2. What did he threaten to do to those who would not obey his order?
3. Why did the three friends refuse to obey the king's command?
4. What was done with them?
5. Why were they unharmed?

# Bible Readings

Are not all angels ministering spirits sent to serve those who will inherit salvation? Hebrews 1:14

When the Son of Man comes in His glory, and all the angels with Him, He will sit on His throne in heavenly glory. Matthew 25:31

He will command His angels concerning you to guard you in all your ways. Psalm 91:11

God did not spare angels when they sinned, but sent them to hell. 2 Peter 2:4

Be self-controlled and alert. Your enemy the devil prowls around like a roaring lion looking for someone to devour. 1 Peter 5:8

# Bible Teachings

The angels are the greatest of God's invisible creatures. They were created holy, but some fell away from God and were condemned to hell. As a result, there are good angels and bad angels.

The good angels are holy spirits. There are multitudes of them, and they are very powerful. They praise God, faithfully carry out His commands, and serve and protect His children.

The bad angels were not faithful to God. There are many bad angels also. They are powerful and cunning. Their leader is Satan. The bad angels spend their time trying to lead God's children into sin and eternal damnation.

# QUESTIONS AND ANSWERS

1. **Did God create invisible creatures?**
   Yes. God created the angels, who are invisible.

2. **Why are the angels invisible?**
   God created the angels to be spirits. Spirits do not have flesh and blood.

3. **Why are there good and evil angels?**
   Led by Satan, some angels rebelled against God. Their minds and wills are now turned against God.

4. **What does the Bible tell us of the good angels?**
   The Bible tells us that the good angels are holy, very numerous, and very powerful.

5. **What blessing do the good angels have?**
   The good angels see God face-to-face and serve Him perfectly.

6. **What great service do they give to God?**
   They carry out God's commands and praise Him. *Angel* means "messenger." They are God's messengers.

7. **How do they help God's children?**
   At God's direction they protect God's people from harm and danger.

8. **What blessings do the good angels bring to you?**
   The good angels are sent by my heavenly Father to watch over me.

9. **Should we pray to the angels?**
   No. We only pray to God. We may pray to God to send His holy angels to take care of us, as Martin Luther did in his Morning and Evening Prayers.

10. **Will I turn into a good angel when I die?**
    No. You will not turn into an angel when you die. You remain your own individual person, although you will have a glorified body.

**11. How did God punish the evil angels?**
He put them out of heaven and condemned them to hell to suffer everlasting punishment.

**12. What do Satan and the evil angels do now?**
They are constantly trying to separate us from God by leading us into sin.

**13. How can we be safe from Satan?**
Jesus has already defeated Satan. Through your faith in Jesus, given to you in your Baptism, you are a new person armed with God's Word and equipped to defeat every temptation of Satan.

# WORD STUDY

*adversary:* enemy; the devil is our adversary

*cunning:* sly; tricky

*to devour:* to swallow up; the devil is trying to devour us

*image:* representation or likeness (e.g., a statue)

*to minister:* to help; to serve

*vigilant:* watchful

Let Your Holy Angel Be Near Me

# Hymn Stanza

Increase, we plead, our song of praise
For angel hosts that guard our days;
Teach us to ceaselessly adore,
To serve as they do evermore.

*LW* 189:4

## Prayer

Heavenly Father, grant, I pray, that Your holy angels may protect and guard me from all evil. Send them to protect me so that the evil angels may not harm me. Hear me for Jesus' sake. Amen.

## What This Means to Me

God made angels to be His messengers and to serve and praise Him. They are His special creation, not people who died and became angels. Some of the angels, led by Satan, fell away from God. It is comforting to me to know that my loving Father in heaven sends His holy angels to protect me everywhere I go. For this kindness I thank God and ask Him to keep His guardian angels near me.

I must remember that Satan and the evil angels are constantly trying to lead me away from God. I know that Jesus has defeated Satan and the evil angels, so I place myself in my Lord's care, knowing that He will give me strength through His Word to resist their wicked temptations.

## God Creates People

*"From one man He made every nation of men."* (Acts 17:26)

# BIBLE STORY

### *How God Created Adam and Eve*

Genesis 1:26–31; 2:1–25

By the sixth day of creation, God had made all of His creatures except one.

Now the LORD God took some earth and formed it in the shape of a man. Then He breathed into his nostrils, giving the man life. God created the man with a soul that can never die and the ability to think. Best of all, God made him holy and without sin, like Himself. The name of this first man was Adam.

Soon afterward God let Adam see and name all the animals He had made. Among all these creatures Adam found none that could be his partner. So God put Adam to sleep, took a rib from his body, and made a woman out of the rib. God brought her to Adam to be his wife, and Adam called her Eve.

God provided a beautiful park, called the Garden of Eden, as the home for Adam and Eve. It was full of wonderful fruit trees and other plants. Here Adam and Eve could live, perfectly holy and happy, and rule over the wonderful world God had created and entrusted to them.

## QUESTIONS FOR DISCUSSION

1. **When did God create the first person?**

2. **In what ways were Adam and Eve higher creatures than the animals?**

3. **In what way were Adam and Eve like God?**

4. **Why were Adam and Eve perfectly happy when God made them?**

## BIBLE READINGS

The LORD God formed the man from the dust of the ground and breathed into his nostrils the breath of life, and the man became a living being. Genesis 2:7

God said, "Let Us make man in Our image, in Our likeness, and let them rule . . . over all the earth." Genesis 1:26

I praise You because I am . . . wonderfully made; Your works are wonderful, I know that full well. Psalm 139:14

Put on the new self, created to be like God in true righteousness and holiness. Ephesians 4:24

✠ [LORD,] I praise You because I am fearfully and wonderfully made. ✠
Psalm 139:14

# BIBLE TEACHINGS

God's greatest visible creatures are human beings. God formed the first person, Adam, out of the earth; He gave him a soul that can never die and the ability to think. God also told him to care for the earth and use it wisely. God also created a partner for Adam, taking special care to provide someone who could establish the first family with Adam. Best of all, God created people in His own image; that is, God made them perfectly holy, like Himself.

# QUESTIONS AND ANSWERS

1. **Why did God give particular attention to the creation of people?**
   Human beings were to be the best and foremost of all God's visible creatures.

2. **How did God make the first human body?**
   God formed the first human body from the dust of the ground.

3. **How did God give man a special kind of life?**
   God breathed into his nostrils the breath of life, and man became a living being (Genesis 2:7).

4. **How did God make it possible for people to rule the earth?**
   God provided people with the ability to reason, to think.

5. **How did Adam, the first person, show the wonderful power of his mind?**
   Adam named the creatures God had created.

6. **Whom did God create as a companion for Adam?**
   God created Eve to be Adam's companion.

7. **Why did Adam name his wife Eve?**
   *Eve* probably means "living." She was to be the mother of all the living.

8. **What was the greatest blessing given to Adam and Eve?**
   Adam and Eve were created in the image of God.

9. **How did the divine image make Adam and Eve the best and foremost of all visible creatures?**
They were like God, holy and righteous; they knew God and were happy in this knowledge.

10. **What was to be the chief work of our first parents?**
In their daily work they were to glorify God for His goodness and to rule over God's creatures. They were to care for the earth.

## WORD STUDY

*dominion:* rule; Adam and Eve were to have dominion over the earth

*image:* likeness

*marvelous:* wonderful

*yield:* bring forth; the earth yields crops

## HYMN STANZA

The Lord, my God, be praised,
My Light, my Life from heaven;
My Maker, who to me
Has soul and body given;
My Father, who will shield
And keep me day by day
And make each moment yield
New blessings on my way.

*LW* 174:1

## PRAYER

O God, almighty Creator of all things, I praise You for Your marvelous works. You have given me a wonderful body and mind. Grant me strength and grace so that I at all times use these gifts to serve You gladly. I pray this in Jesus' name. Amen.

# WHAT THIS MEANS TO ME

I owe my existence to God. Like the psalmist, I, too, must say, "I am fearfully and wonderfully made" (Psalm 139:14). God made me, soul and body. He gave me all my senses and my ability to think. To praise my Creator, I will use and care for these bodily gifts so that I can use them in a full life of service to Him who gave them to me.

*Thanks Be to You, O Lord!*

# UNIT 18  The First Article—Creation

God, the Preserver

*"I will fear no evil, for You are with me."* (Psalm 23:4)

## BIBLE STORY

### *How God Was with Joseph*  Genesis 50:1–20

Joseph's brothers hated him so much that they sold him to slave traders, removing him from their lives forever—so they thought. He was taken to Egypt, where he served for a time in the house of Potiphar, the captain of the king's guards.

God was with Joseph. When Potiphar saw that he could trust Joseph, he made him the caretaker over everything he owned. After Potiphar's wife told wicked lies about Joseph, he was thrown into prison. Again all seemed lost.

Yet God was still with Joseph. With God's help he was able to explain the dreams of the king's butler and baker. When the king also had a dream and no one could explain it, the butler remembered Joseph, who was still in prison. He was quickly brought to Pharaoh, the king, and God gave Joseph the wisdom to tell what the king's dream meant.

Pharaoh then made Joseph a ruler in Egypt. During seven years of very good crops, Joseph directed the gathering of the abundant grain and stored it away for safekeeping for the time when there would be a famine. Then came the seven years of poor crops. Everywhere people were hungry. Only in Egypt there was food—the food that had been stored.

One day Joseph's brothers came to Egypt to buy grain. Joseph recognized them at once. When they came a second time, he forgave the wrong they had done to him. "Go back and get your father and all your families and bring them to Egypt. I will take care of you," Joseph told them.

Because God had watched over Joseph, even the wicked things his brothers had done to him turned out for the best. Joseph said to his brothers, "You intended to harm me, but God intended every thing that happened for good, to accomplish what is now being done, the saving of many lives."

# QUESTIONS FOR DISCUSSION

**1. List the evil things that Joseph experienced.**

**2. Describe how God protected Joseph.**

**3. How is the story of Joseph a picture of how God provided help for people through Jesus?**

# BIBLE READINGS

O LORD, You preserve both man and beast. Psalm 36:6

The eyes of all look to You, and You give them their food at the proper time. Psalm 145:15

No harm will befall you, no disaster will come near your tent. Psalm 91:10

The word of the LORD came to Abram. . . . "Do not be afraid, Abram. I am your shield, your very great reward." Genesis 15:1

In all things God works for the good of those who love Him. Romans 8:28

Give thanks to the LORD, for He is good; His love endures forever. Psalm 118:1

Worship the LORD with gladness; come before Him with joyful songs. Psalm 100:2

# BIBLE TEACHINGS

God gives life, and He preserves it. He gives us everything we need for life. God holds off dangers that threaten us and protects us from evil. Even when we experience something that is evil or bad, God can use it for good for those who love Him.

Although we have done nothing to deserve His love, God is always our loving Father. In His own way and time, He will help us.

By God's power we praise Him for His goodness and gladly serve Him.

# QUESTIONS AND ANSWERS

**1. From whom have you received your life?**
I have received my life from God, my Creator. He used my parents to give me life.

**2. How does God preserve your life?**
God gives me everything I need for my life, including clothing, a home, a sound mind, a healthy body, and strength for my daily tasks.

**3. Since all good things are given to us by God, what should you remember to do?**
I place myself in God's care, trusting that He will give me everything that I need.

**4. How does God show Himself to be the owner of all things and the ruler of the world?**
Though we may not always understand God's ways, He uses people and events for His purposes and shapes them according to His will.

**5. How does God prevent evil from destroying the world?**
By His almighty power, God controls the evil that is in the world. To help control evil, in His Word He has given the commandments. He has also established families and governments to control evil and maintain order.

**6. Why do you, too, need the power of God's protection?**

I am weak and am surrounded by danger and by evil.

**7. How does God's loving care preserve your life?**

God watches over me, defends me, and keeps dangers away from me. Through the power of the Holy Spirit and His Word, God preserves my faith.

**8. Why does God sometimes permit trials to come to you?**

God lovingly strengthens me through these trials and draws me to Himself.

**9. How does God protect your life from evil?**

God provides parents, other adults, and governmental authorities to protect me physically. He protects me spiritually through His Word, which helps me resist the devil's temptations.

**10. Why have we no right to demand good things from God?**

Because of our sinfulness, there is no merit or worthiness in us; we do not deserve God's blessings.

**11. Why, then, does God give us many blessings?**

God blesses us because He is our loving Father. He is a gracious God who blesses His people because He loves them.

**12. What should God's fatherly goodness and mercy lead you to do?**

God's goodness and mercy lead me to trust Him for help and to praise and thank Him for His blessings.

**13. What should God's loving care remove from your heart?**

God's loving care should remove all fear and worry from my heart. Because of my weak faith and sinful heart, I know that at times I worry about things and am afraid; but I know that God still loves me and forgives me for Jesus' sake.

**14. Why may you place yourself in God's care?**

In Jesus, God has kept His promise to provide for my salvation. Since He has also promised to care for me, I trust Him to keep His promises.

**15. How can you show thanks to God for His loving-kindness?**

I can show my thanks to God for His loving-kindness by praising Him and by gladly serving Him in my life.

## WORD STUDY

*abundance:* great plenty
*to chastise:* to punish in order to correct and improve
*merit:* worth; deserving
*to provide:* to take care of
*to sustain:* to support
*trial:* trouble; hardship

## HYMN STANZA

I am Jesus' little lamb,
Ever glad at heart I am;
For my Shepherd gently guides me,
Knows my need and well provides me,
Loves me ev'ry day the same,
Even calls me by my name.

*LW* 517:1

# PRAYER

Dear Father in heaven, my life is in Your hands. Grant me grace and wisdom to see that Your loving-kindness has given me all that I need for my body and life. I am not even aware of some of the harm and danger You have prevented. Show me how to praise You for Your love each day. Help me sing Your praises wherever I go so others will know about Your fatherly goodness and mercy. I pray this in Jesus' name. Amen.

## WHAT THIS MEANS TO ME

I know that the same loving God who made me will watch over me throughout my life. His loving, watchful eye will let no evil harm me. The things that I think are bad God uses for my eternal good. For all this undeserved goodness I praise and serve Him. I pray that God would strengthen my faith so that I trust more and more in God, my mighty Fortress!

# UNIT 19 The Second Article— Redemption

## Jesus Christ, Both God and Man

*"God so loved the world that He gave His one and only Son." (John 3:16)*

I believe in Jesus Christ, His only Son, our Lord, who was conceived by the Holy Spirit, born of the Virgin Mary, suffered under Pontius Pilate, was crucified, died and was buried. He descended into hell. The third day He rose again from the dead. He ascended into heaven and sits at the right hand of God, the Father Almighty. From thence He will come to judge the living and the dead.

*What does this mean?*

I believe that Jesus Christ, true God, begotten of the Father from eternity, and also true man, born of the Virgin Mary, is my Lord,

who has redeemed me, a lost and condemned person, purchased and won me from all sins, from death, and from the power of the devil; not with gold or silver, but with His holy, precious blood and with His innocent suffering and death,

that I may be His own and live under Him in His kingdom and serve Him in everlasting righteousness, innocence, and blessedness,

just as He is risen from the dead, lives and reigns to all eternity.

This is most certainly true.

## BIBLE STORY

### The Birth of Jesus                                    Luke 2:1–14

The little town of Bethlehem was crowded with visitors from all over. Mighty Caesar Augustus, who ruled the Roman world, had commanded all the people to have their

146

names put on tax lists in the hometown of their ancestors. That is why all the descendants of King David went to Bethlehem, the city of David.

Among these descendants was Joseph, a poor carpenter from Nazareth. He arrived in Bethlehem with Mary, his pregnant wife. Every room in the inn was taken; no place was left for them to stay but the stable. Here they made themselves comfortable on the straw as best they could.

That night, in the stable, a son was born to Mary. There was no cradle, and there were no warm blankets. Instead, Mary swaddled her baby tightly in cloths and laid Him in the manger. This baby was the most wonderful baby ever born, for this son of Mary was at the same time the Son of God, the Savior Jesus Christ.

Soon after Jesus was born, a radiant angel of God appeared suddenly to some frightened shepherds in a field near Bethlehem and told them, "Do not be afraid. I bring you good news of great joy that will be for all the people. Today in the town of David a Savior has been born to you; He is Christ the Lord. This will be a sign to you: You will find a baby wrapped in cloths and lying in a manger."

Suddenly with the angel was a multitude of angels, praising God and saying, "Glory to God in the highest, and on earth peace to men on whom His favor rests."

# Questions for Discussion

1. **What brought Joseph and Mary to Bethlehem?**

2. **Why couldn't they find a room in the inn?**

3. **Who was the baby born to Mary?**

4. **Why did He come into the world?**

5. **Why was the news that the angel announced to the shepherds good news?**

# Bible Readings

Salvation is found in no one else, for there is no other name under heaven given to men by which we must be saved. Acts 4:12

You are to give Him the name Jesus, because He will save His people from their sins. Matthew 1:21

God anointed Jesus of Nazareth with the Holy Spirit and power. Acts 10:38

His Son Jesus Christ . . . is the true God and eternal life. 1 John 5:20

There is one God and one mediator between God and men, the man Christ Jesus. 1 Timothy 2:5

# Bible Teachings

*I believe in Jesus Christ, His only Son, our Lord.* These words take us into the heart of the Christian faith. All that we are and hope to be we owe to Jesus.

*Jesus* means "Savior." He deserves that name, for He is our Savior. He saved us from the punishment for our sin—separation from God and eternal life in hell. Jesus is also called the Christ, or the Messiah, because God anointed Him with the Holy Spirit to be our Savior.

Jesus Christ is true God, equal with the Father and the Holy Spirit in every way. He proved this by His mighty works, or miracles. Our Savior is also true man, born of the Virgin Mary. When He was born, He was both fully God and fully man. For that reason He is rightly called the God-Man.

IHS are the first three letters of the Greek word for Jesus (*Iota Eta Sigma*). Many Christians also use these letters to represents the Latin words *Iesus Hominum Salvator*, which means "Jesus, Savior of Men." In this symbol, the Greek *S* looks like a *C*.

## QUESTIONS AND ANSWERS

**1. What chief doctrine of the Christian church is confessed in the opening words of the Second Article?**

In the words *I believe in Jesus Christ, His only Son, our Lord* we confess that Jesus Christ is truly God; this is one of the chief teachings of the Christian faith.

**2. Why did God choose the name *Jesus* for His Son, the Babe of Bethlehem?**

The name *Jesus* tells us that He is the Savior.

**3. Why does Jesus mean so much to you?**

Jesus saved me from hell and assures me heaven, He brought me from death to life, He changed me from being selfish to being loving, and He changed my life from being one of sin to being one of service. That is why Jesus means so much to me.

**4. What does the title *Christ* tell us about Jesus?**

This title tells me that Jesus was anointed to be my Prophet, Priest, and King.

**5. Who is Jesus Christ?**

Jesus Christ is the eternal Son of God who became a human being when He was born in Bethlehem.

**6. Why is Jesus different from all other people?**

Jesus is both true God and true man.

### 7. How do you know that Jesus Christ is true God?

The Bible teaches that Jesus is true God
(1 John 5:20); that Jesus has divine attributes
(John 21:17); and that Jesus does divine works
(Matthew 9:6).

### 8. Why do you believe that Jesus Christ is truly human?

The Bible teaches that Jesus was a human being
(1 Timothy 2:5). He was born of the Virgin Mary
(Luke 2:7) and did human things (John 19:28).

### 9. Why do Christians want all people to know Jesus and believe in Him?

The Bible says that no one will be saved except by
believing that Jesus is the Savior. "Salvation is found
in no one else, for there is no other name under
heaven given to men by which we must be saved"
(Acts 4:12).

### 10. What words could you use to confess that you know Jesus and believe in Him?

I love Jesus as my Savior and follow Him as my
Lord. I'd like to help others know and love Him too.

## WORD STUDY

*to anoint:* to put oil on someone to place them into
an official position

*mediator:* the go-between; Jesus is the go-between
between all people and God.

*miracle:* an extraordinary event caused by God working outside the laws of nature

*multitude:* a great number

*to reconcile:* to make friends again

*tidings:* news

*swaddling clothes:* strips of cloth wrapped tightly
around an infant

# HYMN STANZA

Hark! The herald angels sing,
"Glory to the newborn King;
Peace on earth and mercy mild,
God and sinners reconciled."
Joyful, all you nations, rise;
Join the triumph of the skies;
With angelic hosts proclaim,
"Christ is born in Bethlehem!"
Hark! The herald angels sing,
"Glory to the newborn King!"

*LW* 49:1

*"Glory to God in the Highest!"*

## PRAYER

Dear heavenly Father, I thank You that by Your love I have come to know Jesus as my Savior. Grant me grace that I may trust in Him alone and worship Him as my only Redeemer. For His sake, hear my prayer. Amen.

## WHAT THIS MEANS TO ME

With my whole heart I believe that Jesus Christ, my Savior, is true God and true man. I believe that Jesus, God's only Son, though equal with God the Father, also lived on earth as a true man. As hard to understand as it is, Jesus was and is both God and a human being. He died for me and rose again to save me, things He could do only because He is both God and man. By His grace I will serve Him forever.

# UNIT 20

## The Second Article— Redemption

### The Suffering of the God-Man

*"Look, the Lamb of God,
who takes away the sin of the world!" (John 1:29)*

## BIBLE STORY

### *It Is Finished!* John 18–19

Jesus, the pure and holy Son of God, never sinned. He kept all the commandments of God perfectly. His heavenly Father said about Him, "This is My Son, whom I love; with Him I am well pleased" (Matthew 3:17).

Yet Jesus let Himself be taken prisoner by His enemies. He let them accuse Him of being a wicked criminal, and He permitted Pontius Pilate, the governor, to give the order to nail Him to a cross to be punished like a criminal.

When Jesus hung on the cross, He suffered horrible tortures. His enemies cursed Him; a thief who was crucified with Him mocked Him; and His friends left Him.

Even God the heavenly Father turned away from Him, and Jesus cried, "My God, My God, why have You forsaken Me?" For our sins Jesus suffered all the pains and punishment of hell. When His crucifixion was all over, Jesus shouted these words of victory: "It is finished!"

His suffering was ended. When He died, His wonderful work of redemption was finished. He had done all that was needed to be the Savior of the world. He had taken away the sins of all people. He died at the same hour as the lambs were to be sacrificed in the temple, but He was the Lamb of God who takes away the sin of the world (John 1:29). He had made the final sacrifice for our sins. Indeed, it was finished!

## QUESTIONS FOR DISCUSSION

1. **Why was it important for Jesus to be both God and man?**

2. **For what purpose did Jesus suffer and die?**

3. **Tell what Jesus meant when He said, "It is finished!"**

4. **Explain what the death of Christ means to you.**

## BIBLE READINGS

No one takes [My life] from Me, but I lay it down of My own accord. John 10:18

God made Him who had no sin to be sin for us, so that in Him we might become the righteousness of God. 2 Corinthians 5:21

Christ died for our sins. 1 Corinthians 15:3

For you know that it was not with perishable things

such as silver or gold that you were redeemed . . . but with the precious blood of Christ, a lamb without blemish or defect. 1 Peter 1:18–19

[Christ] died for all. 2 Corinthians 5:15

*"Christ Died for All."*

# BIBLE TEACHINGS

Jesus Christ, true God and true man, is my Lord and Savior. He kept the commandments for me. He suffered under Pontius Pilate and was crucified. This shameful death He suffered not because He *had* to, but because He *wanted* to take away our sin.

The sinless Son of God took our sin upon Himself and suffered our punishment. The Lamb of God shed His holy blood to make us holy and righteous before God.

By His holy life and by His innocent suffering and death, Jesus saved me. What He did for me, He did for all people everywhere.

# QUESTIONS AND ANSWERS

**1. Why do you love Jesus?**
I love Jesus because He is my Savior.

**2. What did Jesus do to be your Savior?**
Jesus kept the commandments for me, and He suffered and died for me.

**3. Why did Jesus suffer and die?**
Jesus suffered and died because of His great love for me and all other people. All people need to have their sins forgiven.

**4. What precious gift have you received through the love of Jesus?**
Jesus has given me freedom from being punished for my sin, being abandoned by God at my death, and being conquered by the devil when he tempts me.

5. **How did Jesus win your freedom?**
As the Lamb of God, Jesus presented Himself to His Father as an offering, a sacrifice, for my sins.

6. **By which acts did Jesus offer Himself to His father?**
Jesus, though true God, became a baby, kept the Father's Law perfectly for me, and then suffered the punishment for my sins.

7. **What was the price Jesus paid to set you free from evil?**
The price Jesus paid was His holy, precious blood.

8. **Why is the blood of Jesus accepted by God as an offering for your sins?**
When Jesus gave His life on the cross, He paid the penalty for sin that God required. His sacrifice fulfilled God's required payment so the sins of all people could be forgiven.

9. **How did Jesus show that He wants all people to be saved?**
Scripture says, "He died for all" (2 Corinthians 5:15). During His life He assured many different kinds of people that their sins were forgiven. He told His disciples to proclaim the Gospel to all people.

10. **How can the blood of Jesus save the whole world?**
It saves everyone because it is the blood of the Son of God.

11. **What does God think of all the people who trust in the blood of Jesus?**
God considers believers to be holy and righteous.

12. **What comforting knowledge does the story of Jesus give you?**
I know that Jesus lived and died for me. Now I know I am a child of God and an heir of salvation.

# WORD STUDY

*blemish:* fault; spot; stain; another name for sin

*corruptible:* not lasting; able to be corrupted

*infinite:* endless

*innocent:* doing no evil

*redemption:* deliverance from sin and eternal death

*sacrifice:* an offering to God

# HYMN STANZAS

My faith looks trustingly
To Christ of Calvary,
My Savior true!
Lord, hear me while I pray,
Take all my guilt away,
Strengthen in ev'ry way
My love for You!

May Your rich grace impart
Strength to my fainting heart,
My zeal inspire;
As You have died for me,
My love, adoringly,
Pure, warm, and changeless be,
A living fire!

*LW* 378:1–2

# PRAYER

My gracious Lord and Savior, You have given Yourself as a sacrifice to take away the sins of all people. I thank You for the indescribable love You have shown to us. I pray, wash my sins away in Your precious blood and make me holy and righteous in Your sight. Amen.

# WHAT THIS MEANS TO ME

"Greater love has no one than this, that he lay down his life for his friends" (John 15:13). Jesus laid down His life for me when He suffered the punishment that I deserved because of my sins. He did this because He loved me. The cross reminds me of the suffering that God's sinless Son took on Himself to make me holy and righteous before God! In thankfulness to Him for His great love to me, I pray that I will praise Him by honoring Him with everything that I do in life.

# UNIT 21

## The Second Article—Redemption

### The Redeeming Death of Jesus

*"By His wounds we are healed."* (Isaiah 53:5)

## BIBLE STORY

### Jesus and the Dying Thief
Luke 23:32–43

Just outside the walls of Jerusalem, at a place called Calvary, stood three crosses. Here the soldiers of Pontius Pilate had crucified Jesus and two thieves. One thief hung to His right and the other to the left.

As people walked by, they laughed at Jesus and shook their heads. "He saved others," they cried, "but He can't save Himself!" They jeered. Even one of the thieves insulted Him.

One of the thieves defended Jesus. He said to the other thief, "Don't you fear God? This Man hasn't done anything wrong. We're getting what we deserve." Then this thief turned to Jesus and said, "Lord, remember me when You come to Your kingdom."

Jesus, His heart full of love, said to the dying thief, "I'm telling you the truth. Today you will be with Me in paradise."

Some time later the thief died and went to heaven with Jesus because he believed that Jesus was suffering and dying for him.

**Today you will be with Me in paradise.**

## QUESTIONS FOR DISCUSSION

**1. Who was crucified with Jesus?**

**2. Contrast how the two thieves treated Jesus.**

**3. How might we at times insult Jesus?**

**4. What does Jesus promise to all who die in faith?**

## BIBLE READINGS

Look, the Lamb of God, who takes away the sin of the world! John 1:29

The blood of Jesus, His Son, purifies us from all sin. 1 John 1:7

Our Savior, Christ Jesus, . . . has destroyed death and has brought life and immortality to light through the gospel. 2 Timothy 1:10

The reason the Son of God appeared was to destroy the devil's work. 1 John 3:8

You were slain, and with Your blood You purchased men for God. Revelation 5:9

Your body is a temple of the Holy Spirit, who is in you. . . . You are not your own. 1 Corinthians 6:19

Where I am, My servant also will be. John 12:26

# BIBLE TEACHINGS

What we buy and pay for belongs to us. Christ has bought us back from the devil with His innocent suffering and death. He has redeemed us. All people now belong to Him. He is rightfully their Lord.

Sin has lost its power because Jesus suffered the punishment for it. Death has lost its sting because Christ died and rose again. What people call death is only a peaceful sleep for the Christian. Satan cannot claim believers as his own because Jesus has taken away all sin.

Believers are the freed children of God, saved to serve Jesus, the Savior, with thankful hearts and to enjoy the glory of heaven with Him when they die.

# QUESTIONS AND ANSWERS

1. **Why do you rightfully belong to Jesus?**
   Jesus has bought me with the great price of His own life and has made me His own child.

2. **What was the price that Jesus paid to redeem you?**
   With His holy precious blood and His innocent suffering and death Jesus redeemed me.

3. **From what has Jesus redeemed you?**
   Jesus has redeemed me from all sins, from death, and from the power of the devil.

4. **For what purpose has Jesus redeemed you?**
   Jesus has redeemed me so that I might be His own, live under Him in His kingdom, and serve Him.

5. **Why do you gladly serve Jesus?**
   Jesus has been kind and good to me. He loves me.
   He is my deliverer from sin and its consequences.

6. **Why is it foolish to serve the devil and those who follow him?**
   The devil and his followers are cruel and deceitful;
   they will separate me from my Savior. They are not
   interested in my eternal salvation.

7. **Why is it wrong to live for yourself only?**
   A selfish life is not Christlike; Jesus gave His life for
   me. In response, I want to live to praise Him.

8. **How might you lovingly serve Christ?**
   I can serve Jesus by worshiping Him and by helping
   other people for His sake.

# WORD STUDY

*to abolish:* to do away with

*to crucify:* to nail to a cross

*deceitful:* tricky; misleading

*immortality:* endless life; living forever

*to manifest:* to make known

# HYMN STANZA

Chief of sinners though I be,
Jesus shed His blood for me,
Died that I might live on high,
Lives that I might never die.
As the branch is to the vine,
I am His, and He is mine.

*LW* 285:1

## PRAYER

I thank You, Lord Jesus, that You have redeemed me and made me Your own child. Help me to love You more and more each day. Take me into Your care and help me to care for others. Amen.

## WHAT THIS MEANS TO ME

With Jesus as my Savior I have nothing to fear. His holy, precious blood has freed me from the guilt of sin, the terror of death, and the deceitful and deadly power of the devil. Now I am God's own child. I can serve Him during my life here on earth and live eternally with Him in heaven after I die.

# UNIT 22　　The Second Article—
# Redemption

## The Resurrection
## and Ascension of Jesus

*"Thanks be to God! He gives us the victory through our Lord Jesus Christ." (1 Corinthians 15:57)*

# BIBLE STORY

### *Jesus' Resurrection and Ascension*　　　　　John 20:1–25; Mark 16:1–20

Jesus died on the cross on Good Friday afternoon. Some of His friends took Him down from the cross and laid Him in a nearby grave.

Early the next Sunday morning, just as the sun was rising, James's mother Mary, Mary Magdalene, and Salome, friends of Jesus, walked sadly toward His grave. They wanted to anoint the body of Jesus with sweet spices. "Who will move the big stone away from the opening to the grave?" was the question the women discussed as they walked.

As they came close to the grave, they were surprised to discover that the stone was already rolled away from the opening. They hurried to the grave and found—not Jesus—but a young man dressed in a snow-white garment— an angel. Where was Jesus? The women were filled with fear.

"Don't be afraid," the angel said. "You are looking for Jesus of Nazareth, who was crucified. He has risen! Go and tell His disciples, and especially Peter, what you have seen! Tell them they can see Jesus in Galilee."

During the next 40 days Jesus often talked with His friends and ate with them. His appearances showed that He was truly risen from the dead. At the end of 40 days He took them to a mountain near Jerusalem. He said to them, "Go into all the world and preach the Gospel to every creature. Those who believe will be saved and those who do not believe will be condemned."

As He was talking with them, He began to ascend. Higher and higher He went until a cloud hid Him and His disciples could no longer see Him. Jesus had ascended into heaven to rule with God the Father and the Holy Spirit.

## QUESTIONS FOR DISCUSSION

1. **What did the women expect to find at the grave?**

2. **What did the angel say to them?**

3. **What happened on the 40th day after Christ's resurrection?**

4. **What great command did Jesus give to His disciples?**

5. **How can people today carry out the directions that Jesus gave to His disciples at His ascension?**

# BIBLE READINGS

[Christ] was raised on the third day according to the Scriptures. 1 Corinthians 15:4

[Jesus] was delivered over to death for our sins and was raised to life for our justification. Romans 4:25

Because I live, you also will live. John 14:19

After the Lord Jesus had spoken to them, He was taken up into heaven and He sat at the right hand of God. Mark 16:19

All authority in heaven and on earth has been given to Me. Matthew 28:18

Surely I am with you always, to the very end of the age. Matthew 28:20

# BIBLE TEACHINGS

Christ died for our sins, but He did not stay in the grave. On the third day He became alive again. His descent into hell and His resurrection showed that He was the victor over sin, death, and the devil.

By rising from the dead, Christ proved that He is truly the Son of God and the Savior of the world. Because He rose from the dead, we, too, shall rise.

After appearing to His disciples during the 40 days after Easter, Jesus ascended into heaven to rule over the world and especially to care for those who trust in Him.

# Questions and Answers

**1. What great victory did Jesus win on Easter Day?**
On the third day when He rose again from the dead, Jesus won the victory over sin, death, and the devil.

**2. What does the resurrection of Jesus prove?**
The resurrection of Jesus proves that Jesus is truly the Son of God and the Savior of the world.

**3. What should we remember when we are sad and discouraged?**
Christ's victory over death and the devil is our own victory. His victory encourages us when we are sad and discouraged; it brings us consolation.

**4. Which wonderful promise of Jesus will be fulfilled for all believers?**
For all believers Jesus' promise, "because I live, you also will live," will be fulfilled in heaven (John 14:19).

**5. To whom did Jesus show Himself after the resurrection?**
Jesus showed Himself to His friends and many other people (1 Corinthians 15:6).

**6. Why did Jesus show Himself to His friends?**
Jesus appeared to them to strengthen their faith in His resurrection.

**7. Why is Christ's resurrection important?**
"If Christ has not been raised, your faith is futile; you are still in your sins" (1 Corinthians 15:17).

**8. What happened on the 40th day after Christ's resurrection?**
Forty days after His resurrection, Jesus ascended into heaven.

**9. Where is Jesus now?**
As the Apostles' Creed indicates, Jesus is sitting at the right hand of God the Father almighty. As true God, He is present everywhere.

**10. How is Jesus now using His divine power?**
Jesus now rules the world as the glorious King of kings.

11. **What comfort is there in knowing that Jesus is the King of kings?**

Jesus, the King, is our Savior; He takes special care of His people.

12. **What brings Christians great joy in this life and in eternity?**

To live under Him in His kingdom brings Christians great joy.

# Word Study

*consolation:* comfort

*disciple:* a pupil or follower

*justification:* declaring the sinner not guilty

*offense:* another name for sin

*resurrection:* rising from the dead

*victor:* winner

# Hymn Stanzas

I know that my Redeemer lives!
What comfort this sweet sentence gives!
He lives, He lives, who once was dead;
He lives, my ever-living Head!

He lives, all glory to His name!
He lives, my Savior, still the same;
What joy this blest assurance gives:
I know that my Redeemer lives!

*LW 264:1, 8*

"*Christ is Risen!*"

# PRAYER

Blessed Jesus, You are the Prince of life and the Lord of glory. I adore You for winning the victory over death and the devil. Be near me always with Your love and care. Give me faith to believe that, by Your power, I, too, will rise from the dead. Increase my trust in Your love and take me at last to heaven, where I will see You face-to-face. Amen.

# WHAT THIS MEANS TO ME

In His Word, the Bible, God has given me the message that Jesus rose from the dead and ascended to heaven, yet He is always present with me and rules the world in wisdom and glory! This risen Jesus is my Savior. On a day known only to Him, He will call me to Himself in heaven. On the Last Day, He will unite my resurrected body with my soul. He is even now in heaven and on earth watching over me and all those who trust in Him.

> Christ the Lord is ris'n on high; Alleluia!
> Now He lives no more to die. Alleluia!
>
> *LW* 137:2

# UNIT 23

## The Second Article—Redemption

### The Last Judgment

*"He will reign for ever and ever."* (Revelation 11:15)

## BIBLE STORY

### How Jesus Will Judge All People

Matthew 25:31–46

Shortly before His suffering and death, Jesus told His disciples that He would come to judge the living and the dead.

As Jesus describes it, the Last Day will be a wonderful day for those who trust in Him as their Savior. On the Last Day of the world Jesus will come in all His glory as the King of heaven, and all His holy angels will come with Him. Jesus will sit on His throne, and all the people then living, as well as all the millions that have ever lived, will stand before Him. You will not be able to count everyone who is present.

Jesus will put all the believers on His right hand, and all the unbelievers He will place on His left. "Come, you who are blessed by My Father," Jesus will say to those on His right, "take your inheritance, the kingdom prepared for you since the creation of the world. For I was hungry, and you gave Me something to eat. I was thirsty and you gave Me something to drink. I was a stranger and you invited Me in. I needed clothes and you clothed Me. I was sick and you looked after Me. I was in prison and you came to visit Me."

"When did we do that? We do not remember that at all," the righteous will ask.

"Every time you were kind to anyone who needed help, you were doing it for Me," Jesus will say.

How different His words to the unbelievers will be! "I was hungry and thirsty, a stranger needing clothes, sick and in prison, and you never helped Me. You must go to the punishment of hell forever," He will say.

"But, Lord, we never had a chance to do anything for You!" they will cry. "When did we see You hungry, or thirsty, or a stranger needing clothes, or sick, or in prison, and did not help You?"

Jesus will answer, "Every time you had a chance to help someone in trouble and failed to do so, you refused to do it for Me."

## QUESTIONS FOR DISCUSSION

1. **When will Jesus come back to earth?**

2. **Why will He come?**

3. **How do the children of God show that they love Him?**

4. **How do the unbelievers show that they do not love God?**

5. **Do people get to heaven because they do good things?**

# Bible Readings

This same Jesus, who has been taken from you into heaven, will come back in the same way you have seen Him go into heaven. Acts 1:11

No one knows about that day or hour, not even the angels in heaven, not the Son, but only the Father. Mark 13:32

When these things [the signs before the Last Day] begin to take place, stand up and lift up your heads, because your redemption is drawing near. Luke 21:28

When the Son of Man comes in His glory, and all the angels with Him, He will sit on His throne in heavenly glory. Matthew 25:31

[God] has set a day when He will judge the world with justice by the Man He has appointed. He has given proof of this to all men by raising Him from the dead. Acts 17:31

# Bible Teachings

On the Last Day, which is known only to God, our Savior will come back as the King of Glory to judge all people, the living and the dead.

This will be a terrible day for those who do not believe in Jesus as their Savior, but it will be a most happy day for all the children of God. On that day Jesus will condemn the unbelievers to hell, but He will take the believers to the heavenly home that His heavenly Father has prepared for them. In heaven God's people, those who love and trust Him, will live in His presence forever. What a wonderful Savior we have!

# QUESTIONS AND ANSWERS

1. **When will we see Jesus?**
   We will see Jesus with our eyes on the Last Day of the world and in all eternity.

2. **When will be the Last Day?**
   Only God knows when the Last Day will be.

3. **How will Jesus come on the Last Day?**
   Jesus will come in all His glory, and all the holy angels will come with Him.

4. **For what purpose will Jesus come on the Last Day?**
   Jesus will come to judge the living and the dead.

5. **Why did Jesus not judge the world immediately after His resurrection?**
   Jesus wanted the Gospel to be preached throughout the world.

6. **Why will Judgment Day be a terrible day for unbelievers?**
   On that day Jesus will send unbelievers to everlasting punishment.

7. **Why will Judgment Day be a day of joy for believers?**
   On that day Jesus will take believers to the heaven that He and His Father have prepared for them.

8. **Since we do not know when Judgment Day will be, what can we do to be ready?**
   We can be watchful so that we do not give in to the devil's temptations; we can also pray that God the Holy Spirit would preserve our faith during these days.

9. **How can we be watchful?**
   We can use God's Word as a guide for our lives, and, by God's grace, follow His commandments and receive His pardon for our sins.

10. **How might praying help us be ready for the Last Day?**
    In our prayers we can ask Jesus to keep us in true faith and to help us love others.

**11. What are some activities that we might do with special zeal while there is still time?**

One thing we might do is proclaim the Gospel to as many people as possible, providing the Holy Spirit with the opportunity to win souls for Christ.

The ichthus is one of the earliest Christian symbols. It features a fish because the first letters of the phrase *Jesus Christ, Son of God, Savior* formed the word *fish* in Greek.

## Word Study

*frame:* body

*Judgment Day:* the Last Day

*to ordain:* to appoint

*redemption:* deliverance

## Hymn Stanza

Let us also live with Jesus.
　　He has risen from the dead
That to life we may awaken.
Jesus, since You are our head,
We are Your own living members;
　　Where You live, there we shall be
In Your presence constantly,
　　Living there with You forever.
Jesus, let me faithful be,
　　Life eternal grant to me.

*LW* 381*:4

# Prayer

Blessed Lord Jesus, when You first appeared on earth, You came to save me. At Your second appearing, You will come to judge me. I pray, prepare me for Your coming on the Last Day so that I will be ready to meet You as my Lord and King. Come, Lord Jesus; come quickly. Amen.

## What This Means to Me

I do not know when Jesus will come to call me home, but I believe He is my Savior. By His grace I will live so that I am ready to go with Him at any time. Firmly believing that my sins are washed away in His blood, I will eagerly look forward to that glorious day when I will meet Him face-to-face. In this life my goal will be to do those things that please Jesus and bring glory to His name. I will try not to do anything that I would be ashamed to be doing when Jesus comes to take me home; rather, I will serve Him by helping others with the talents and gifts He has given me.

*"Come, Lord Jesus!"*

# UNIT 24     The Third Article—
## Sanctification

## The Holy Spirit

*"I will pour out My Spirit on your offspring,
and My blessing on your descendants."* (Isaiah 44:3)

> I believe in the Holy Spirit, the holy Christian
> church, the communion of saints, the forgiveness
> of sins, the resurrection of the body, and the life
> everlasting. Amen.

### What does this mean?

I believe that I cannot by my own reason or strength
believe in Jesus Christ, my Lord, or come to Him; but the
Holy Spirit has called me by the Gospel, enlightened me with
His gifts, sanctified and kept me in the true faith.

In the same way He calls, gathers, enlightens, and sanctifies the whole Christian church on earth, and keeps it with
Jesus Christ in the one true faith.

In this Christian church He daily and richly forgives all
my sins and the sins of all believers.

On the Last Day He will raise me and all the dead, and
give eternal life to me and all believers in Christ.

This is most certainly true.

## BIBLE STORY

### How the Holy Spirit Came to the Disciples
Acts 2:1–41

"I will send the Holy Spirit to you," Jesus told His
disciples a little while before He ascended into heaven.
Ten days later the disciples were meeting together in a
house in Jerusalem, as they did every day, waiting for
their Lord's promise to be fulfilled.

On this day the sound of a rushing, mighty wind from heaven suddenly filled the whole house. At the same time small flames of fire could be seen above their heads. Most surprising of all, the disciples began to proclaim the wonderful works of God in many languages—languages they had never spoken before.

Many people from all parts of the world heard them and asked, "What's going on? How can these men speak to us in our own language?"

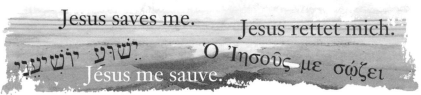

Jesus saves me.　Jesus rettet mich.
יֵשׁוּעַ יוֹשִׁיעֵנִי　Ὁ Ἰησοῦς με σώζει
Jésus me sauve.

Peter stood up and explained, "What you are seeing is the pouring out of the Holy Spirit, as God promised long ago. Jesus of Nazareth did many wonderful things to prove that He is the Son of God, as all of you know. He was handed over to you, and you put Him to death by nailing Him to a cross. God, however, raised Him from the dead. This is what we have seen. Now He rules in heaven and is pouring out the Holy Spirit, as you see now."

The people took Peter's sermon to heart. "What can we do?" they asked.

"Be sorry for your sins," Peter said, "and be baptized in the name of Jesus Christ for the forgiveness of your sins. Then you will receive the gift of faith from the Holy Spirit. This promise is meant for you and for your children."

On that day about three thousand people became believers.

# Questions for Discussion

1. The festival of the Holy Spirit is called Pentecost. What does *Pentecost* mean?

2. What did the sound of the wind and the flames of fire indicate?

3. Who gave the disciples the power to speak in different languages? Why was this ability given to the disciples?

4. How did the people become Christians?

5. What messages are there in the story of Pentecost for Christians today?

# Bible Readings

The man without the Spirit does not accept the things that come from the Spirit of God, for they are foolishness to him. 1 Corinthians 2:14

No one can say, "Jesus is Lord," except by the Holy Spirit. 1 Corinthians 12:3

Restore me, and I will return, because You are the LORD my God. Jeremiah 31:18

Come to Me, all you who are weary and burdened, and I will give you rest. Matthew 11:28

God, who said, "Let light shine out of darkness," made His light shine in our hearts. 2 Corinthians 4:6

[God] called you to this through our Gospel, that you might share in the glory of our Lord Jesus Christ. 2 Thessalonians 2:14

Faith comes from hearing the message, and the message is heard through the word of Christ. Romans 10:17

We are God's workmanship, created in Christ Jesus to do good works, which God prepared in advance for us to do. Ephesians 2:10

[You] through faith are shielded by God's power until the coming of the salvation that is ready to be revealed in the last time. 1 Peter 1:5

The inspired Apostle Paul once wrote, "No one can say, 'Jesus is Lord,' except by the Holy Spirit" (1 Corinthians 12:3). Without the Holy Spirit's work, therefore, we are helpless; we cannot understand anything about Jesus Christ, our Savior; we can do nothing to believe in Him and be saved.

Since the fall into sin, by nature our hearts are filled with unbelief and hatred toward God.

Only the Holy Spirit, who is true God with the Father and the Son, can change our hearts. He invites and urges us to come to Jesus; He creates saving faith in us, enabling us to believe in Jesus as our Savior. He gives us power to live as God wants us to live. He also keeps us in the faith. This is what is meant by the statement, "The Holy Spirit sanctifies us." The Spirit makes us holy before God through faith in Christ.

The Holy Spirit does all His wonderful work through the Gospel. The Gospel is the power of God to give salvation to everyone who believes.

**The Word for the World**

# QUESTIONS AND ANSWERS

1. **What does St. Paul mean when he says, "No one can say, 'Jesus is Lord,' except by the Holy Spirit"?**

   Paul meant that only the Holy Spirit has the power to enable a person to believe that Jesus is the Savior and Lord.

2. **Why can't we believe in Jesus by our own reason or strength?**

   Since the fall into sin, all human beings, in spiritual matters, are blind and dead and opposed to God.

3. **How does the Holy Spirit bring us to faith in Jesus?**

   The Holy Spirit creates faith in people so that they believe that Jesus Christ loves them and that He died for them.

4. **Where is the story of Christ's love to be found?**

   The story of Christ's love is to be found in the Gospel of Jesus, given to us in the Bible.

5. **How does the Holy Spirit use the Gospel of Jesus Christ?**

   By means of the Gospel of Jesus Christ, the Holy Spirit invites, or calls, us to believe in Jesus.

6. **Why is the Gospel called the power of God for salvation?**

   Through the Gospel the Holy Spirit makes us able and willing to believe in Jesus and to love Him.

7. **What great miracle does the Holy Spirit work in you through the Gospel of Jesus Christ?**

   Through the Gospel the Holy Spirit changes my heart and enlightens my mind, so that I see and love Jesus as my personal Savior.

8. **What marvelous changes has the word of the Gospel brought about in you?**
I was dead, but now I live; I was blind, but now I see; I was helpless, but now I am strengthened; I hated God and people, but now love lives in my heart.

9. **For what other purpose does the Holy Spirit use the Gospel?**
The Holy Spirit gives me power to lead a godly life and keeps me in the true faith until my end.

10. **Why is the Gospel God's most precious gift to you?**
The Gospel gives me faith in Christ and thus makes me holy before God. Only through the Gospel can I be a member of God's family, serve Him here on earth, and live with Him eternally in heaven.

# WORD STUDY

*communion of saints:* all people who believe in Jesus Christ

*Pentecost:* the 50th day after Easter

*to persuade:* to urge someone to believe or do something

*to reveal:* to make known

*to sanctify:* to make holy

*God's workmanship:* what God has made

# HYMN STANZAS

Come, Holy Ghost, God and Lord,
With all Your graces now outpoured
On each believer's mind and heart;
Your fervent love to them impart.
Lord, by the brightness of Your light
In holy faith Your Church unite;
From ev'ry land and ev'ry tongue
This to Your praise, O Lord, our God, be sung:
Alleluia, alleluia!

Come, holy Fire, comfort true,
Grant us the will Your work to do
And in Your service to abide:
Let trials turn us not aside.
Lord, by Your pow'r prepare each heart,
And to our weakness strength impart
That bravely here we may contend,
Through life and death to You,
    our Lord, ascend.
Alleluia, alleluia!

*LW* 154:1, 3

## PRAYER

O Holy Spirit, You make known the deep things of God. I thank You that You have led me to faith in Jesus as my Savior. Help me to show my faith by a holy life, and keep me in Your truth to my life's end. Grant me these blessings for Jesus' sake. Amen.

## WHAT THIS MEANS TO ME

I could never believe what Jesus has done for me if God's Holy Spirit had not called me by the Gospel and led me to know and love my Savior. God has sent His Holy Spirit to bring me to the loving arms of Jesus! Now I pray that God would send His Holy Spirit to live in my heart, to sanctify my life, and to keep me in the true faith until He calls me home to heaven.

# UNIT 25 — The Third Article—Sanctification

## The Holy Christian Church, the Communion of Saints

*"Christ loved the church and gave Himself up for her."*

*(Ephesians 5:25)*

## BIBLE STORY

### Christ's Promise to Build His Church

Matthew 16:13–20

Our Lord Jesus spoke many wonderful words and did many wonderful deeds. Everyone who heard or saw Him developed ideas about Him.

One day, when Jesus was alone with His disciples, He asked them, "Who do people say the Son of Man is?"

"Some say that You are John the Baptist," they told Him. "Some say You are Elijah, and others say You are Jeremiah or some other prophet."

"Who do you say I am?" Jesus asked.

Simon Peter, speaking for all the disciples, answered, "You are the Christ, the Son of the living God!"

This answer pleased Jesus. "You are blessed," He said to Peter. "This truth was taught to you by My Father in heaven. You are Peter [Peter means rock], but on this rock [the truth that you confessed] I will build My church; and the gates of hell [all the powers of the devil] will not overpower it."

## QUESTIONS FOR DISCUSSION

**1. Explain the words that Peter said to Jesus.**

**2. What did Jesus promise to His church?**

**3. Which church is Christ's church today?**

## BIBLE READINGS

On this rock I will build My church, and the gates of Hades will not overcome it. Matthew 16:18

The Lord knows those who are His. 2 Timothy 2:19

No one can lay any foundation other than the one already laid, which is Jesus Christ. 1 Corinthians 3:11

[You] are . . . fellow citizens with God's people and members of God's household, built on the foundation of the apostles and prophets, with Christ Jesus Himself as the chief cornerstone. Ephesians 2:19–20

# BIBLE TEACHINGS

All believers in Christ are brothers and sisters in the family of God. We call this family the holy Christian church, or the communion of saints.

The church has been compared to a building in which Christ is the foundation. The church is also called a body, of which Christ is the head.

The church is holy because all its members are saints in God's sight, cleansed of all their sins by the blood of Christ.

Only God knows who the members of His church are; He alone can look into the hearts of people and see whether or not they believe.

Those who are members of the holy Christian church, members of God's holy family, share all the blessings that God gives His children.

# QUESTIONS AND ANSWERS

**1. Who are God's holy people?**
All believers in Christ are God's holy people.

**2. How are all believers in Christ related to one another?**
All believers in Christ are brothers and sisters in the family of God.

**3. By what name do we know the family of God?**
We know the family of God as the holy Christian church, or the communion of saints.

**4. Why is the church called the communion of saints?**
Saints are people who are cleansed of all their sins by the blood of Christ. Since a communion is a group of people, the communion of saints is a group of people who believe that Jesus has taken their sins away and express their thankfulness to Him in their lives.

**5. Why should no one in the church think himself better than others?**
All are sinners, and all are cleansed by Jesus' blood.

**6. Who is the head of the church?**
The head of the church is Jesus Christ.

**7. Why do you want to be a member of God's holy family?**
As a member of God's holy family I share in all the blessings that God gives to His children.

**8. How do you become a member of the holy Christian church?**
I become a member of the holy Christian church through faith in Jesus Christ.

**The Ark of the Church**

**9. What are some benefits of joining a Christian congregation?**
In a Christian congregation I will have opportunity to learn more about Jesus and His love for me. I will also be able to have my faith strengthened in the Sacrament of the Altar. Through a Christian congregation I can help proclaim God's Word to others and come to know Christian friends.

**10. Which Christian congregation should you join?**
I plan to join only a congregation that teaches the Word of God in its truth and purity and administers the Sacraments correctly.

**11. What are some ways that you can thank God that He has made you a member of the holy Christian church?**
I could support the work of the church with my prayers, time, talents, and money. I could also become a full-time church worker, such as a pastor, teacher, director of Christian education, director of Christian outreach, missionary, deaconess, or church musician.

# WORD STUDY

*congregation:* a group of people who worship together

*foundation:* the base on which a building stands

*Hades:* hell

*loyal:* true; faithful

*to prevail:* to gain the victory

*to proclaim:* to make known

*Son of Man:* Jesus' favorite name for Himself;
this name states He was truly human;
Jesus' messianic title

*talent:* ability

*unity:* being joined together, as in one body

# HYMN STANZA

The Church's one foundation
Is Jesus Christ, her Lord;
She is His new creation
By water and the Word.
From heav'n He came and sought her
To be His holy bride;
With His own blood He bought her,
And for her life He died.

*LW* 289:1

**The Rock of Salvation**

# PRAYER

Father in heaven, through the Holy Spirit's power You have gathered all believers together and made them one in Your church. Grant me and my fellow believers a strong faith so that we may remain unified in the Spirit and, together with all Your holy people, share in Your blessings to the church and teach and proclaim Your Good News to everyone. I pray this through Jesus Christ, the Lord and head of the church. Amen.

# WHAT THIS MEANS TO ME

It is a privilege for me to be a member of God's holy family, the holy Christian church, and to share in all the blessings that God gives to His children! I plan to join a congregation that supports preaching and teaching the Word of God in its truth and purity, and I will support it with my prayers, time, talents, and money.

Since I appreciate the blessings of the Gospel, I will help my fellow members of Christ's church proclaim and teach the message of salvation in Christ to others who do not know of His love.

# UNIT 26

## The Third Article—Sanctification

### The Forgiveness of Sins

*"The Lord is full of compassion and mercy."* (James 5:11)

## BIBLE STORY

### *God's Greatest Gift to His Church*     Mark 2:1–12

The city of Capernaum on the northwest shore of the Sea of Galilee was a favorite city of the Lord Jesus. He often went there to preach and heal the sick.

One time when Jesus went to Capernaum, the people heard about His arrival and hurried to the house where Jesus was staying. They came to hear and to see Him. "Perhaps He will do something wonderful again," they said.

Soon no one else could get in the house because it was so crowded. Outside was a group of four men who wanted to see Jesus. They were carrying a very sick friend on a bed. He could not move his arms or legs, and he suffered terrible pain. His friends knew that Jesus could help.

When they saw that they could not get through the door of the house, they carried the man, in his bed, up to the flat roof of the house. Then they removed some of the roof tiles and lowered their sick friend through the opening until he was right in front of Jesus.

When Jesus saw their strong faith in Him, He said to the sick man, "Your sins are forgiven." When some teachers from the synagogue accused Him of blasphemy because they knew only God could forgive sins, Jesus also healed the man's sick body. Jesus knew that sin is the greatest trouble of all and that forgiveness of sin is the most wonderful blessing. It is the greatest gift that He could give. He wanted everyone to know that, because He was God, He had the power to forgive sins and to heal the body.

## QUESTIONS FOR DISCUSSION

1. **What did the people of Capernaum do when they heard that Jesus was in the city?**

2. **Why did one group of men go to the house where Jesus was?**

3. **How did they get their sick friend to Jesus?**

4. **What is the greatest gift Jesus can give?**

5. **Is it easy for you to forgive people who have wronged or hurt you? Should you forgive them? Why or why not?**

# BIBLE READINGS

Praise the Lord, O my soul, and forget not all His benefits—who forgives all your sins. Psalm 103:2–3

In [Jesus Christ] we have redemption through His blood, the forgiveness of sins, in accordance with the riches of God's grace. Ephesians 1:7

With You there is forgiveness. Psalm 130:4

By grace you have been saved, through faith— and this not from yourselves, it is the gift of God. Ephesians 2:8

[The jailer asked,] "What must I do to be saved?"

They replied, "Believe in the Lord Jesus, and you will be saved." Acts 16:30–31

Take heart, son; your sins are forgiven. Matthew 9:2

# BIBLE TEACHINGS

In the forgiveness of sins God gives people the one thing that is needed the most and that can bring eternal joy. Even though God's children love their Savior, because of their weakness they still sin each day. As a result, God's people need forgiveness of their sins each day in order to remain His children.

In His mercy God gives what is needed. Daily and richly He forgives all sin, as He has promised in His Word: "I . . . will remember their sins no more" (Jeremiah 31:34).

People can do nothing to earn forgiveness of sins. Christ, our Savior, has already earned complete forgiveness for all sin. The ancient church used the symbol of the pelican as a symbol for Jesus Christ. The pelican may give its own flesh and blood for its young to eat so that the young pelicans can survive, just as Christ gave His blood to save His people. Now God grants each person forgiveness as a free gift. By God's grace I trust God's promise with all my heart and rejoice that I am saved by grace.

## QUESTIONS AND ANSWERS

1. **Why is the forgiveness of sins the greatest blessing in the world?**
   The forgiveness of sins brings us into God's family as His children.

2. **Why do even Christians need forgiveness of sins?**
   Christians need forgiveness of sins because they, too, sin every day.

3. **Why can't our good works earn forgiveness for our sins?**
   Since all our righteous acts are like filthy rags (Isaiah 64:6), even our supposedly good actions could never earn forgiveness of sins from God.

4. **Who alone has earned forgiveness of sins for us?**
   Christ, our Savior, has earned forgiveness of sins for us.

5. **Through what means does God offer forgiveness as a free gift?**
   Through the Gospel of Jesus Christ God offers forgiveness as a free gift.

6. **When do we receive the forgiveness that God offers?**
   We receive forgiveness when we believe God's promise, "I will remember [your] sins no more" (Jeremiah 31:34).

**7. How do we become willing and able to believe God's promise?**

By using God's Word, the Holy Spirit creates faith in our heart that believes the promises of God.

**8. What are some responses that believers have to God's forgiveness?**

In response to God's forgiveness, Christians often are humble in the light of God's love, thankful for His mercy, and filled with joy at His care.

**9. Why do Christians have no right ever to be boastful and proud?**

Every Christian must confess, "I am saved by grace alone."

**10. Although Christians may fall into despair because of their constant sinning, what assurance does God provide?**

God's Word assures us that God daily and richly forgives all sins to all believers.

**11. How may you show your thankfulness for the grace of God?**

I can tell others about the mercies of God.

**12. Why do we desire to share the Gospel?**

Christians want everyone to turn from darkness to light, to receive forgiveness of sins.

# WORD STUDY

*blasphemy*: speaking evil of God or treating Him with contempt or irreverence; mocking God

*crimson:* deep red color, almost like purple

*to despair:* to lose hope

*grace:* undeserved kindness; God's Riches At Christ's Expense

*iniquities:* sins

*penitent:* sorry for having done wrong

# Hymn Stanza

I lay my sins on Jesus,
The spotless Lamb of God;
He bears them all and frees us
From the accursed load.
I bring my guilt to Jesus
To wash my crimson stains
Clean in His blood most precious
Till not a spot remains.

*LW* 366:1

# Prayer

My dear God and Father, I am not worthy to be called Your child, because every day I sin in thought, word, and deed. For Jesus' sake forgive all my sins. Increase my trust in Your grace so that I might be Your child forever. Amen.

# What This Means to Me

I sin every day. Although I try to avoid sin and walk more closely with Jesus, my sins are still with me. I am thankful that, as a child in God's holy family, I receive full and complete forgiveness for all my sins every day! This great gift I receive through faith in Jesus from my forgiving Father in heaven.

# UNIT 27 The Third Article Sanctification

## The Resurrection of the Body and the Life Everlasting

*"In My Father's house are many rooms."* (John 14:2)

## BIBLE STORY

### The Rich Man and Poor Lazarus    Luke 16:19–31

A rich man lived in a large, beautiful home. He wore the finest, most expensive clothes. With his friends he enjoyed tasty foods every day. He had everything that money could buy, and he used his riches for his own pleasure.

At the same time a poor, sick beggar named Lazarus lay in the street outside the rich man's door. His whole body was covered with painful sores. Lazarus hoped to get a few crumbs from the rich man's table, but the rich man did not help Lazarus. Only dogs came and licked his sores.

One day Lazarus died, and the holy angels carried him to Abraham's side in heaven, the eternal dwelling place of the righteous people of God.

The rich man also died and was buried, but he went to hell.

# Questions for Discussion

1. **Tell about the difference between the rich man and Lazarus in this life.**

2. **After the two men died, where was each one taken?**

3. **Why did these men arrive at two different places? (See Mark 16:16.)**

4. **What were some points Jesus was making for us when He told this parable?**

# Bible Readings

A time is coming when all who are in their graves will hear His voice and come out—those who have done good will rise to live, and those who have done evil will rise to be condemned. John 5:28–29

[Christ] will transform our lowly bodies so that they will be like His glorious body. Philippians 3:21

You have made known to me the path of life; You will fill me with joy in Your presence, with eternal pleasures at Your right hand. Psalm 16:11

I tell you the truth, today you will be with Me in paradise. Luke 23:43

I desire to depart and be with Christ, which is better by far. Philippians 1:23

# Bible Teachings

This world will someday come to an end. On that day God will make all dead people alive again. Unbelievers will be sent to hell, to live separated from God for eternity.

Believers, however, will rise to everlasting life in heaven. Heaven is the eternal home of God's people. In heaven believers will have the same body they had on earth, but it will be perfect—free from all sin, pain, and death. With body and soul united again, believers will be with Christ in joy and live in glory without end.

# Questions and Answers

**1. Why do we believe in the resurrection of the body?**

God has promised to raise our bodies. His promise is sure, for with God all things are possible (Matthew 19:26).

**2. What body will the believers have in heaven?**

The believers will have the same body they had on earth.

**3. How will their bodies be different in heaven from what they were on earth?**

In heaven their bodies will be perfect; they will be free from all sin, pain, and death (1 Corinthians 15:42–43).

**4. Whose body will our resurrection body resemble?**

Our resurrection body will be like Christ's glorious body (Philippians 3:21).

**5. When they rise from the dead, what difference will there be between believers and unbelievers?**

The believers will rise with glorified bodies to everlasting life in heaven; the unbelievers will rise to everlasting damnation.

**6. What is the most glorious part of being in heaven?**

The most glorious part of being in heaven is that believers will be with Christ forever. This is the greatest joy of heaven.

**7. Why are you sure that you will see God face-to-face in heaven?**

I trust that Jesus is my Savior, who has assured the forgiveness of all my sins. God is faithful; all His promises, including those to forgive my sins for Jesus' sake, are sure.

**8. Why are you especially thankful to God the Holy Spirit?**

God the Holy Spirit has created faith in me and has preserved this faith through which I obtain eternal life.

9. **How may we show that we think of heaven as our real home?**

Since heaven is my real home, I thank God for all the blessings He gives me as I live on earth, but I look forward to living in heaven.

10. **Why is it important to study God's Word, participate in the Sacraments, and worship God faithfully as we live here on earth?**

The Bible says, "With You is the fountain of life; in Your light we see light" (Psalm 36:9). Only through God's Word can we see the light of the Gospel of Jesus Christ, our Savior and Redeemer.

## WORD STUDY

*dayspring:* beginning of day (used of Jesus)

*to fashion:* to make; God fashions us to be His people

*to inherit:* to receive as a gift from one's father

*paradise:* another name for heaven

*resurrection:* rising from the dead

*summons:* call

*vile:* unclean; very bad; as a result of sin, we are vile

# Hymn Stanzas

O Morning Star, how fair and bright!
You shine with God's own truth and light,
Aglow with grace and mercy!
Of Jacob's race, King David's Son,
Our Lord and Master, You have won
Our hearts to serve You only!
Lowly, holy!
Great and glorious,
All victorious,
Rich in blessing!
Rule and might o'er all possessing!

What joy to know, when life is past,
The Lord we love is first and last,
The end and the beginning!
He will one day, oh, glorious grace,
Transport us to that happy place
Beyond all tears and sinning!
Amen! Amen!
Come, Lord Jesus!
Crown of gladness!
We are yearning
For the day of Your returning.

*LW* 73\*:1, 5

# Prayer

Lord Jesus Christ, You have ascended to heaven to prepare a place for us. Help us, by Your Holy Spirit, to remain steadfast in true faith and to dwell with You in paradise when we die. Amen.

# WHAT THIS MEANS TO ME

Confidently believing the sure promise of God, I need have no fear of death and the grave. I know that when I die, I will be asleep in Jesus. On Judgment Day He will awaken my body and reunite it with my soul in heaven. Lovingly my Savior will welcome me and all believers with the words, "Come, you who are blessed by My Father; take your inheritance, the kingdom prepared for you since the creation of the world" (Matthew 25:34). There I will live eternally in the presence of the Holy Trinity.

I believe this with all my heart because God's promises are sure.

# UNIT 28 The Introduction to the Lord's Prayer

*"Lord, teach us to pray." (Luke 11:1)*

Our Father who art in heaven, hallowed be Thy name, Thy kingdom come, Thy will be done on earth as it is in heaven. Give us this day our daily bread; and forgive us our trespasses as we forgive those who trespass against us; and lead us not into temptation, but deliver us from evil. For Thine is the kingdom and the power and the glory forever and ever. Amen.

*Our Father in heaven, hallowed be Your name, Your kingdom come, Your will be done on earth as in heaven. Give us today our daily bread. Forgive us our sins as we forgive those who sin against us. Lead us not into temptation, but deliver us from evil. For the kingdom, the power, and the glory are Yours now and forever. Amen.*

## THE INTRODUCTION

Our Father who art in heaven.
*Our Father in heaven.*

*What does this mean?*
With these words God tenderly invites us to believe that He is our true Father and that we are His true children, so that with all boldness and confidence we may ask Him as dear children ask their dear father.

# BIBLE STORY

### *Abraham's Prayer for Sodom*     Genesis 18:16–33

Not far from the home of Abraham was the city of Sodom, where Abraham's nephew Lot and his family lived. The people of Sodom were very wicked and ungodly.

One day the Lord God visited Abraham and told him that He would soon destroy Sodom. Abraham at once thought of Lot and asked God, "Are You going to destroy the good people along with the wicked? What if there are 50 righteous people living in Sodom."

"If I find 50 righteous people there, I will spare all the people," said the Lord.

"I really don't have a right to speak to You, Lord, " continued Abraham, "but will You destroy the city if there are 45 righteous people living there?"

"No, if there are 45 righteous ones in the city, I will not destroy it," the Lord replied.

"What if there are 40?" asked Abraham.

"I will spare the city for the sake of the 40," God said.

"Do not be angry, Lord, if I speak again," Abraham said, "but what if there are 30?"

"I will not destroy it if I find 30 there," God answered.

"What if there are 20?" asked Abraham.

"I will not destroy it for the sake of 20 either," God answered.

"O Lord," Abraham said, "don't be angry if I ask once more. What if there are at least 10 righteous ones living there?"

"I will not destroy it for the sake of 10," God said.

Then the Lord went His way, and Abraham returned home.

## QUESTIONS FOR DISCUSSION

1. **Why did God want to destroy Sodom?**

2. **How did Abraham try to change God's mind?**

3. **How often did Abraham ask God to spare Sodom?**

4. **How did God show His willingness to listen to Abraham?**

5. **What does this conversation tell us about God?**

## BIBLE READINGS

You, O LORD, are our Father, our Redeemer from of old is Your name. Isaiah 63:16

May the words of my mouth and the meditation of my heart be pleasing in Your sight, O LORD, my Rock and my Redeemer. Psalm 19:14

When you pray, do not keep on babbling like pagans. Matthew 6:7

I want men everywhere to lift up holy hands in prayer, without anger or disputing. 1 Timothy 2:8

Pray continually. 1 Thessalonians 5:17

I urge, then, first of all, that requests, prayers, intercession and thanksgiving be made for everyone. 1 Timothy 2:1

I tell you the truth, My Father will give you whatever you ask in My name. John 16:23

Ask and it will be given to you. Matthew 7:7

Lord, teach us to pray. Luke 11:1

## Bible Teachings

God is our heavenly Father, and, by His grace, we are His beloved children. God invites us to talk with Him as children talk freely with their father. Such heart-to-heart talking with God is prayer. Saying words with our lips only is no prayer.

God wants us to pray everywhere, at all times, and for all people on earth, even for our enemies. We may ask for anything good.

Our heavenly Father has promised to hear us whenever we pray in the name of Jesus and according to His will. When He does not give us what we ask, He gives us something better or is saying, "That is not good for you at this time."

The best prayer is the Lord's Prayer, which the Lord Jesus taught to His disciples. In this prayer our Savior Himself teaches us how to pray.

# QUESTIONS AND ANSWERS

**1. What is a prayer?**
A prayer is talking with God.

**2. Why should we pray often?**
We need God's help at all times, especially in times of trouble.

**3. Why have we a right to pray to God?**
God is our true Father, and we are His true children by faith in Jesus Christ. He has invited and urged us to pray to Him.

**4. Where does God want us to pray?**
God wants us to pray everywhere, especially when we are alone. He also wants us to pray with others, with our family at home, with our friends, or with the members of our congregation during worship services.

**5. When does God want us to pray?**
God wants us to pray at all times. He invites us to pray especially every morning and evening, before and after meals, and in times of trouble and temptation.

**6. For whom does God want us to pray?**
God wants us to pray for ourselves and others, for our friends and loved ones, for the poor and the sick, and for our enemies.

**7. For what may we ask God in our prayers?**
We may ask God for everything that is to His glory and to our good.

**8. Why may we pray with great confidence?**
God has encouraged us to pray and has promised to answer our prayers in ways that are for the good of His people.

**9. In what three ways may God answer prayer?**
He may say Yes, No, or Wait.

**10. When does God say Yes?**
God answers our prayers with Yes when what we ask for, in His eyes, is good for us or His kingdom.

**11. When does God say No?**
God says No to our prayer when what we ask for, in His judgment, is not good for us or His kingdom.

**12. When does God say Wait?**
God answers our prayer with Wait when what we ask for, in His eyes, will be good for us at some later time.

**13. What prayer was given to the Christian church as a model prayer?**
The Lord's Prayer is Christ's model prayer given to the Christian church.

**14. Why is it called the Lord's Prayer?**
The Lord Himself gave it to His disciples and to us.

**15. What are three parts of the Lord's Prayer?**
The three parts of this prayer are the Introduction, the Seven Petitions, and the Conclusion.

**16. What is the Introduction?**
The Introduction is the opening sentence, in which we speak to God as our Father.

**17. What do we ask of our Father in the first three petitions?**
In these petitions we ask for heavenly blessings.

**18. What do we ask of our Father in the Fourth Petition?**
In this petition we ask for earthly blessings.

**19. What do we ask of our Father in the last three petitions?**
In these last petitions we ask for deliverance from sin and evil.

**20. How do we conclude the Lord's Prayer?**
We say, "For Thine is the kingdom and the power and the glory forever and ever. Amen."

**21. By what name do we call on the triune God in the Lord's Prayer?**
In this prayer we use the name *Father* to address God.

**22. Why would God have us address Him as *our Father?***
In these words God invites us to speak with Him as children speak to a father who loves them.

**23. With what feelings should we pray to God?**
We should pray to Him with boldness and confidence.

**24. What does it mean to pray to God with boldness?**
We pray with boldness when we pray to Him without fear. We know we can be bold in our prayers because we know God loves us and wants to help us in ways that are best for us and His people.

**25. When do we pray to God with all confidence?**
We pray with confidence when we are sure that He will hear us and help us in ways that He knows are best.

# Word Study

*ceasing:* stopping; to pray without ceasing means the Christian life is a life of prayer

*confidence:* trust

*to exhort:* to urge

*intercession:* pleading for another

*meditation:* quiet thought; Christian meditation is based on God's Word

*to petition:* to ask

*privilege:* a special right

*sincere:* honest

*ungodly:* disobeying or denying God; not living according to God's Law

*vain:* empty, useless, worthless

# HYMN STANZAS

What a Friend we have in Jesus,
All our sins and griefs to bear!
What a privilege to carry
Ev'rything to God in prayer!
Oh, what peace we often forfeit;
Oh, what needless pain we bear -
All because we do not carry
Ev'rything to God in prayer!

Have we trials and temptations?
Is there trouble anywhere?
We should never be discouraged -
Take it to the Lord in prayer.
Can we find a friend so faithful
Who will all our sorrows share?
Jesus knows our ev'ry weakness—
Take it to the Lord in prayer.

*LW* 516:1–2

## PRAYER

Dear Father in heaven, You have told me to pray, and You have promised to hear me when I pray. Lead me by Your Holy Spirit to talk with You about all the things that concern me and lead me to ask You for the things I think I need. Give me those gifts that are good for me. I ask this because Jesus Christ is my Savior. Amen.

## WHAT THIS MEANS TO ME

As a child of God I can speak to my heavenly Father freely and often. He has promised to hear and answer me every time I pray in the name of Jesus. To receive the fullness of God's blessings, I pray continually, using God's Word for guidance and asking the Holy Spirit to help me pray.

# UNIT 29     The First Three Petitions

Praying for Spiritual Blessings

*"Seek first His kingdom and His righteousness."*
*(Matthew 6:33)*

## THE FIRST PETITION

Hallowed be Thy name.

*Hallowed be Your name.*

*What does this mean?*
God's name is certainly holy in itself, but we pray in this petition that it may be kept holy among us also.

*How is God's name kept holy?*
God's name is kept holy when the Word of God is taught in its truth and purity, and we, as the children of God, also lead holy lives according to it. Help us to do this, dear Father in heaven! But anyone who teaches or lives contrary to God's Word profanes the name of God among us. Protect us from this, heavenly Father!

## THE SECOND PETITION

Thy kingdom come.

*Your kingdom come.*

*What does this mean?*
The kingdom of God certainly comes by itself without our prayer, but we pray in this petition that it may come to us also.

*How does God's kingdom come?*
God's kingdom comes when our heavenly Father gives us His Holy Spirit, so that by His grace we believe His holy Word and lead godly lives here in time and there in eternity.

# THE THIRD PETITION

Thy will be done on earth as it is in heaven.
*Your will be done on earth as in heaven.*

*What does this mean?*
The good and gracious will of God is done even without
our prayer, but we pray in this petition that it may be
done among us also.

*How is God's will done?*
God's will is done
> when He breaks and hinders every evil plan and pur-
> pose of the devil, the world, and our sinful nature,
> which do not want us to hallow God's name or let
> His kingdom come;
> and when He strengthens and keeps us firm in His
> Word and faith until we die.

This is His good and gracious will.

## BIBLE STORY

### *How the Christians Prayed for the Church*

Acts 4:1–31

At the time when our Lord Jesus ascended into
heaven, the Christian church was very small. The congregation in Jerusalem had only about 120 members. Peter,
John, and the other apostles, by the power of the Holy
Spirit, preached about Jesus and of His resurrection from
the dead. Many people believed in Jesus and became

members of the Christian church. Soon there were 5,000 Christians in Jerusalem.

Many powerful enemies confronted the Christians during these early years. The leaders of the Jewish people especially hated Jesus and His church. They tried everything in their power to destroy Christianity.

One day Peter and John were arrested and ordered to stop preaching about Jesus. Peter and John said, "We cannot stop. We must talk about the things that we have seen and heard."

"If you will not stop this preaching, you will be punished," the Jewish leaders said.

Peter and John went to the Christian congregation and told them everything that had happened. When they heard the report, the whole congregation joined in a beautiful prayer for the church: "Lord, You are the God who made the heaven and the earth, the sea and all things. The same powerful enemies who hated Your holy child, Jesus, and crucified Him are now threatening to destroy Your church. We pray, give Your servants the strength and courage to preach Your Word. Support their preaching with miracles. In Jesus' name we pray."

When they finished their prayer, they were all filled with the Holy Spirit, ready to preach about Jesus without fear.

## QUESTIONS FOR DISCUSSION

1. **How big was the Christian church after Jesus' ascension into heaven?**

2. **Describe some measures the enemies of the church took to try to destroy it.**

3. **For what did the Christian congregation pray?**

4. **What was God's answer to their prayer?**

5. **What does God want the church of today to do?**

## BIBLE READINGS

Let the [prophet] who has My word speak it faithfully. Jeremiah 23:28

Let your light shine before men, that they may see your good deeds and praise your Father in heaven. Matthew 5:16

The kingdom of God is near. Repent and believe the good news. Mark 1:15

Do not be afraid, little flock, for your Father has been pleased to give you the kingdom. Luke 12:32

God our Savior . . . wants all men to be saved. 1 Timothy 2:3–4

It is God's will that you should be sanctified. 1 Thessalonians 4:3

## BIBLE TEACHINGS

**First Petition.** Jesus instructs us to pray for spiritual gifts. Therefore, in the Lord's Prayer, we first ask God to help us keep His name holy by teaching His Word clearly and faithfully and by empowering us to lead a holy life. In this petition we also pray that God would preserve us from the disastrous effects of false teachings and unholy lives.

**Second Petition.** In this petition we ask our Lord to keep us in His kingdom by creating and preserving in us faith in Jesus, our Savior. We also pray that He will make us eager to spread His saving Word and to lead others to faith in Jesus and to membership in the Christian church.

**Third Petition.** Our heavenly Father knows what is best for us. His will is always right. We pray that He may help us do His will cheerfully, as the angels do in heaven. To this end we pray that God will also stop the evil efforts of the devil, the world, and our sinful heart to destroy our faith. In this petition we pray that God would keep us faithful until we die.

# QUESTIONS AND ANSWERS

1. **What do we ask of our Father in the First Petition?**
   In this petition we pray, "Hallowed be Thy name."

2. **By whom is the name of God always kept holy?**
   The name of God is always kept holy by the angels in heaven.

3. **By whom should God's name likewise be hallowed?**
   God's will is that all people on earth hallow His name.

4. **How is God's name hallowed?**
   God's name is hallowed in two ways: (1) when the Word of God is taught in its truth and purity, and (2) when we, as the children of God, also lead holy lives according to it.

5. **When is God's Word taught in its truth and purity?**
   God's Word is taught truthfully and purely when nothing is added to it, nothing is taken away, and its meaning is not changed from what God intended.

6. **What do we show when we lead a holy life?**
   When we lead a holy life, we show that we are God's children.

7. **What will other people do when they see the good life of Christians?**
By God's power they will praise and honor His name.

8. **Why do Christians earnestly pray, "Help us do this, dear Father, in heaven"?**
Without God's help Christians cannot teach the Bible as God wants it taught, nor can they live the kind of life God wants them to live.

9. **How is God's Word profaned?**
God's Word is profaned when something impure is added to it, when something is taken away, or when its meaning is changed. God's name is also profaned when someone claims to be a Christian but leads an evil life.

10. **What happens to the name of God if we live in sin and shame?**
The name of God is disgraced and dishonored among people.

11. **Regarding false doctrine and ungodly life, what is the prayer of the Christian church?**
Christians pray, "Protect us from this, heavenly Father."

12. **What do we ask of our Father in the Second Petition?**
We pray, "Thy kingdom come."

13. **What is your greatest blessing?**
I have been delivered from the kingdom of Satan and have been made a citizen of God's kingdom of grace.

14. **Where is God's kingdom of grace found?**
God's kingdom of grace is found wherever the Gospel of Jesus Christ is preached.

15. **Who are the citizens of the kingdom of God?**
All those who believe the Gospel are citizens of the kingdom of God.

16. **How has God made you a citizen of His kingdom?**
God has made me a citizen of His kingdom by bring-
ing the Gospel to me in His Word. In my Baptism He
created faith in my heart, making me a citizen in His
kingdom.

17. **How does our heavenly Father enable us to believe?**
Our heavenly Father creates faith in our hearts by
using the power of His Holy Spirit.

18. **What precious gift do we receive from the Holy
Spirit?**
By His grace we receive the power to believe God's
Word of forgiveness through Jesus.

19. **Why do we need the grace of God?**
We need His grace because by ourselves we are unable
to believe the Word of our King.

20. **How do we show that we are citizens of God's
kingdom?**
Citizens of God's kingdom lead godly lives, here in
time and in eternity.

21. **Why is God's kingdom called the kingdom of grace?**
In His kingdom God operates only by grace, that is,
by His undeserved mercy.

22. **Why do we say, "The kingdom of God certainly
comes by itself without our prayer"?**
We cannot do anything to bring the kingdom of God
to ourselves. As sinful people, we do not even want to
pray that God's kingdom would come to us.

**Thy Will Be Done**

**23. Why, then, do we pray that the kingdom of God should come?**

Those who know from God's Word that they are sinful plead with God to be gracious to them through Jesus. They also pray that God's kingdom would come to all people.

**24. What should we do so that the kingdom of God may come also to others?**

In this Second Petition we ask that God would spread His kingdom throughout the world. Believers support this effort by actively sharing the Gospel with others and by supporting the work of Christian missionaries. Believers do this by giving their time, talents, and treasures to this mission.

**25. How long will God's kingdom of grace endure?**

This kingdom will endure to the end of the world.

**26. Which kingdom do believers enter when they die?**

When believers die, they enter the kingdom of glory.

**27. Why do believers look forward to the kingdom of glory with joy?**

In heaven we shall see our King in all His glory and be able to serve Him perfectly forever.

**28. How long will God's kingdom of glory endure?**

God's kingdom of Glory will endure throughout eternity.

**29. What do we ask of our Father in the Third Petition?**

We pray, "Thy will be done on earth as it is in heaven."

**30. What is the good and gracious will of God?**

His good and gracious will is that all people believe in Christ and be saved.

**31. How is God's will done?**

God's will is done when believers hallow God's name because they are citizens of His kingdom.

**32. How does God show His great love and mercy?**
God shows His mercy when He forgives our sin for Jesus' sake. God also shows His mercy when He showers His blessings on everyone, good and evil alike; when rain waters everyone's fields; when sun makes everyone's plants grow; and when governments maintain order. These blessings come to us even when we do not pray for them.

**33. Why, then, should we pray, "Thy will be done"?**
Believers should pray "Thy will be done" because they know that they are fallen creatures who have been redeemed by Jesus Christ. Only God knows what is good and right for all people. By praying this phrase, Christians place everything into God's hands and ask that God's good and gracious will may be done among us and by us.

**34. Whose evil counsel and will are opposed to God's will?**
The counsel and will of the devil, the world, and our evil heart are all opposed to God's will.

**35. With what words might we ask God to protect us from those who want to harm us?**
We could pray that God would conquer and defeat every plan and purpose of the devil, of people in the world who want to do evil, and of our own sinful nature.

**36. How will God help us to overcome the evil counsel and will?**
Through the power of the Holy Spirit given in Word and Sacrament, God will strengthen and preserve us in faith until we die.

# WORD STUDY

*counsel:* plan; plot

*to hallow:* to keep holy

*to profane:* to treat with contempt

*sanctification:* holiness; leading a godly life

*seraphim:* angels of high rank

*triumphant:* victorious

# Hymn Stanzas

Our Father, who from heav'n above
Has told us here to live in love
And with our fellow Christians share
Our mutual burdens and our prayer,
Teach us no thoughtless word to say
But from our inmost heart to pray.

Your name be hallowed. Help us, Lord,
In purity to keep Your Word
That to the glory of Your name
We walk before You free from blame.
Let no false teaching us pervert;
All poor deluded souls convert.

*LW* 431:1–2

# Prayer

Dear heavenly Father, help me keep Your name
holy. Give me Your Spirit so that I may grow in faith and
lead others into Your kingdom. Grant me grace to do
Your will, and keep me faithful throughout my life. Hear
my prayer for Jesus' sake. Amen.

# What This Means to Me

Jesus wants God to be of first importance in my life.
He has the best opportunity to be supremely important
in my life when I do the following:

+ Read and hear His Word diligently;

+ Ask the Holy Spirit to guide me in all I do;

+ Do God's will cheerfully and gladly; and

+ Seek first the kingdom of God.

By God's grace honoring the First Commandment
will be the chief aim in my life.

# UNIT 30    The Fourth Petition

Praying for Daily Bread

*"You open Your hand and satisfy the desires of every living thing."* (Psalm 145:16)

Give us this day our daily bread.

*Give us today our daily bread.*

*What does this mean?*
God certainly gives daily bread to everyone without our prayers, even to all evil people, but we pray in this petition that God would lead us to realize this and to receive our daily bread with thanksgiving.

*What is meant by daily bread?*
Daily bread includes everything that has to do with the support and needs of the body, such as food, drink, clothing, shoes, house, home, land, animals, money, goods, a devout husband or wife, devout children, devout workers, devout and faithful rulers, good government, good weather, peace, health, self-control, good reputation, good friends, faithful neighbors, and the like.

## BIBLE STORY

### How God Fed His People in the Wilderness    Exodus 16:1–31

For about 400 years the people of Israel were slaves in Egypt. Then God led them out of Egypt. He brought them safely through the Red Sea and protected them from Pharaoh's army.

When the people came to the wild and barren country east of the Red Sea, they found nothing to eat. Soon they began to complain, "Oh, if only we had stayed in Egypt. At least there we had plenty to eat! Here we have no food! We're going to starve."

"I have heard the cries of the people," God said to Moses. "I will feed them. I will let bread drop like rain from heaven. Everyone will have enough to eat every day. Every morning there will be bread to gather."

And so it was. Every morning the ground was covered with small round pieces of bread that looked like frost. The people called the bread *manna*, which means "What is it?"

Moses told them, "This is the bread that the Lord has given you to eat."

For 40 years the people of Israel lived in the wilderness, and in all that time God never failed to send them bread from heaven.

## QUESTIONS FOR DISCUSSION

1. **Why was there no food for the people of Israel?**

2. **How did God provide food to the people?**

3. **What did the people call the bread from heaven?**

4. **Who gives you your daily bread? Give some examples.**

# BIBLE READINGS

The eyes of all look to You, and You give them their food at the proper time. Psalm 145:15

He causes His sun to rise on the evil and the good, and sends rain on the righteous and the unrighteous. Matthew 5:45

If a man will not work, he shall not eat. 2 Thessalonians 3:10

Do not forget to do good and to share with others. Hebrews 13:16

Give me neither poverty nor riches, but give me only my daily bread. Proverbs 30:8

Do not worry about tomorrow. Matthew 6:34

Give thanks to the LORD, for He is good; His love endures forever. Psalm 106:1

# BIBLE TEACHINGS

All that we have is a gift of our God. In His great love God showers His blessings on all people, believers and unbelievers alike.

Jesus teaches us to pray to God for our daily bread so that we may

&#8224; remember that our food and all other possessions come from God;

&#8224; thank God for His goodness and mercy;

&#8224; willingly and honestly do our work each day;

&#8224; be satisfied with what God gives us; and

&#8224; be ready to share our blessings with others.

# QUESTIONS AND ANSWERS

**1. What do we ask of our Father in the Fourth Petition?**

We ask God to give us this day our daily bread.

**2. How does God, as a rule, give us our daily bread?**

He gives us skills so that we can earn our daily bread through the work we do.

**3. How might some people receive their daily bread dishonestly?**

Some people might obtain it by stealing, by fraud, or in other dishonest ways.

**4. Why does God give us daily bread even when we forget to ask for it?**

God gives daily bread to us, and even to the wicked, out of fatherly, divine mercy.

**5. Why, then, do we pray in this petition that God give us our daily bread?**

We pray this petition so that we are reminded each day that our blessings come from God, by His grace, and so that we then receive our daily bread with thanksgiving.

**6. When is an especially good time to give thanks to God for our daily bread?**

An especially good time to give thanks to God for our daily bread is before and after meals.

**7. What is meant by "daily bread"?**

Our daily bread is every gift God gives to us by which He cares for us. These gifts include the food we eat, our homes and families, friends, good government, good weather, safe places to live, and the like.

**8. Why do we say *this day* and *daily*?**

These words remind us that God cares for us every day; His love for us is everlasting.

9. **Why do we not have to worry about what will happen in the future?**
We are always in God's hands. He has promised that He will supply all our needs.

10. **How might we show our gratefulness to God for the blessings He gives us?**
We might worship Him as the giver of every good and perfect gift. When we help those in need, we also are thanking God for His gifts.

# WORD STUDY

*convenient:* fit; suitable; proper
*devout:* God-fearing
*flourish:* grow abundantly
*gratefulness:* thankfulness
*meat:* another word for food
*poverty:* being poor
*spouse:* husband or wife
*take no thought:* do not worry

# HYMN STANZA

Feed Your children, God most holy,
Comfort sinners poor and lowly;
You our Bread of Life from heaven,
Bless the food You here have given!
As these gifts the body nourish,
May our souls in graces flourish
Till with saints in heav'nly splendor
At Your feast our thanks we render.

*LW* 468

# PRAYER

O God, from whom all blessings flow, I thank You for the food, clothing, and shelter You have given me. I pray, protect my loved ones who take care of me. Bless those who rule our country and keep peace among the nations of the earth. By Your love shown to me through Jesus, my Savior, move me to share my blessings with others. Through Jesus Christ, my Lord, I pray. Amen.

## WHAT THIS MEANS TO ME

When I pray for daily bread, I am asking God to give me the things I need to live and be happy. For these blessings I need to give God daily thanks. As part of my thankfulness, I will be satisfied with what God gives me. I pray that I will always be willing to share my blessings with those in need.

# The Last Three Petitions and the Conclusion

Praying for Deliverance

*"The LORD will watch over your coming and going."*
*(Psalm 121:7)*

## THE FIFTH PETITION

And forgive us our trespasses, as we forgive those who trespass against us.

*Forgive us our sins as we forgive those who sin against us.*

*What does this mean?*

We pray in this petition that our Father in heaven would not look at our sins, or deny our prayer because of them. We are neither worthy of the things for which we pray, nor have we deserved them, but we ask that He would give them all to us by grace, for we daily sin much and surely deserve nothing but punishment. So we too will sincerely forgive and gladly do good to those who sin against us.

## THE SIXTH PETITION

And lead us not into temptation.

*Lead us not into temptation.*

*What does this mean?*

God tempts no one. We pray in this petition that God would guard and keep us so that the devil, the world, and our sinful nature may not deceive us or mislead us into false belief, despair, and other great shame and vice. Although we are attacked by these things, we pray that we may finally overcome them and win the victory.

# THE SEVENTH PETITION

But deliver us from evil.

*But deliver us from evil.*

*What does this mean?*
We pray in this petition, in summary, that our Father in heaven would rescue us from every evil of body and soul, possessions and reputation, and finally, when our last hour comes, give us a blessed end, and graciously take us from this valley of sorrow to Himself in heaven.

# THE CONCLUSION

For Thine is the kingdom and the power and the glory forever and ever. Amen.

*For the kingdom, the power, and the glory are Yours now and forever. Amen.*

*What does this mean?*
This means that I should be certain that these petitions are pleasing to our Father in heaven, and are heard by Him; for He Himself has commanded us to pray in this way and has promised to hear us. Amen, amen means "yes, yes, it shall be so."

# BIBLE STORY

### *How God Delivered Paul from Evil*
2 Timothy 4:6–8; 17–18

The Apostle Paul was a prisoner in a dark jail in Rome.

Many years had passed since he had become a believer in Jesus. All that time he had dearly loved his Lord and Savior. He had traveled thousands of miles by land and sea, labored and suffered, just so he could speak to as many people as possible about Jesus and His love for people as shown through His suffering, death, and resurrection.

Now, however, Paul was in chains in prison. Enemies of Jesus had managed to have Paul arrested and brought to Rome. He was sure that he would never be free to travel again. He was certain that in a very short time he would be put to death—a martyr for Jesus.

Yet Paul had a positive attitude while he was in prison. He remembered that God had often protected him in the past. As his mind went back over all the many evils that he had suffered, he remembered how God had helped him through every single one of them. He thought, for example, of how God had saved him in a shipwreck. On the island of Malta, he had been bitten by a poisonous snake, but God had saved his life. His confidence that God had delivered him from sin and death through the Savior, Jesus Christ, brought him special joy.

No wonder that just before his death Paul could say, "The Lord will rescue me from every evil attack and will bring me safely to His heavenly kingdom. To Him be glory for ever and ever. Amen" (2 Timothy 4:18).

# Questions for Discussion

**1. What was Paul's great work?**

**2. Why was he put in prison?**

**3. What brought him joy in prison?**

**4. Why was Paul ready and willing to face death?**

**Merciful God**

# Bible Readings

God, have mercy on me, a sinner. Luke 18:13

When you stand praying, if you hold anything against anyone, forgive him, so that your Father in heaven may forgive you your sins. Mark 11:25

My son, if sinners entice you, do not give in to them. Proverbs 1:10

Watch and pray so that you will not fall into temptation. Matthew 26:41

We must go through many hardships to enter the kingdom of God. Acts 14:22

The Lord will rescue me from every evil attack and will bring me safely to His heavenly kingdom. To Him, be glory for ever and ever. Amen. 2 Timothy 4:18

# BIBLE TEACHINGS

Sin is the greatest evil. All our troubles come from sin. Jesus teaches us to ask God to forgive all our sins for Jesus' sake. God's complete forgiveness brings us joy and empowers us to gladly forgive those who have wronged us.

As long as we live, we will be tempted to sin against God and to desert our faith. That is why we pray to God, asking Him to keep us safe from every temptation and to give us strength to remain faithful every time we are tempted.

Because of sin this world is full of evil. There is much suffering. The children of God, too, suffer many sorrows and troubles. God urges His people to ask Him to help them conquer evil temptations and to deliver them safely to Himself in heaven.

# QUESTIONS AND ANSWERS

1. **For what do we pray in the Fifth Petition?**
   We pray in this petition that our Father in heaven would not see our sin when He looks at us.

2. **What would happen if God did see our sins?**
   When God sees our sin, He must punish us. Without Jesus' suffering and death in our place, we are God's enemies.

3. **Why wouldn't God give us the things we ask for if He would see our sin?**
   Since He would then see us as sinners, we would not be worthy of the things for which we pray; we simply would not deserve to have our prayers answered.

4. **What plea must we make to God when we ask Him to answer our prayers?**
   We ask Him to give us what we ask by grace, for Jesus' sake, who suffered and died for our sins and rose from the dead.

5. **Why must we expect everything by grace?**
Since every day we sin and deserve nothing but punishment, we receive God's answers to our prayers only because of His gracious love for us.

6. **Since God, by grace, for Jesus' sake, forgives us our sins, how do we as faithful children of God respond when someone sins against us?**
Because we are forgiven by God, we readily forgive others and do good to those who sin against us.

7. **What do we ask of our Father in the Sixth Petition?**
We pray that He would not lead us into temptation.

8. **Does God ever tempt anyone to commit sin?**
God never tempts anyone to sin, but God does permit trials to come to us in order to strengthen our faith in Him and love for others.

9. **Since God tempts no one, why then do we pray to Him, "Lead us not into temptation"?**
We are really praying that God would guard and protect us so that the devil, the world, and our sinful nature may not mislead us.

10. **How does the devil tempt us?**
The devil tempts us by putting wicked thoughts into our minds. Some people around us (the world) may try to get us to do wicked things or to say ugly things to others. Some people are wicked examples for others. Some activities and entertainments try to make evil activities look harmless, popular, or attractive. The devil has many ways to tempt us to sin against God.

11. **What will these enemies succeed in doing if we do not watch and pray?**
These enemies will lead us away from God and the activities that please Him. Jesus pictures these enemies as leading us away from Him, getting us to lose our trust in Him, leading us to despair of ever being saved, and doing shameful things (vices).

**12. To whom do we turn for help to resist temptation?**
Jesus is the only one who can help us. By His resurrection He has already conquered sin, death, and the devil. In our prayers we ask Him to stand by our side so that we may overcome all temptations and share in the victory He won for us on the cross.

**13. What do we ask of our Father in the Seventh Petition?**
We pray, "Deliver us from evil."

**14. Why might we say that the last petition is the most important one of all?**
When, by God's grace, we are delivered from evil, we are safe and secure for time and for eternity.

**15. From what evils do we ask God's protection?**
In this petition we ask God to deliver us from every evil that may afflict our body and soul, property, and reputation.

**16. How does God deliver us from affliction?**
In His wisdom God either takes the cross from us or He gives us strength to bear it patiently.

**17. When is this prayer especially important?**
It is especially important to be delivered from evil when the time of our death is near.

**18. Why is the time of our death a serious moment?**
It is at that moment that Jesus looks into our heart to determine whether or not we trust in Him as our Savior. On that basis He frees us from the devil's temptation and takes us to heaven or we are plunged into the greatest of all evils, eternal death.

**19. Who is your Savior from evil?**
My Lord Jesus Christ saves me from evil.

**20. What did Christ do to save you?**
Christ lived and died for me and rose again.

21. **What will be your earnest cry when your last hour has come?**
Lord Jesus, grant me a blessed end, and graciously take me to be with You in heaven.

22. **What is the Conclusion of the Lord's Prayer?**
For Thine is the kingdom and the power and the glory forever and ever. Amen.

23. **Why do we conclude the Lord's Prayer with these words of praise?**
With these words we praise God, our King, who controls all things and who hears our prayers and is able to answer them in ways that are for our eternal good.

24. **What great truth does the concluding word *Amen* announce?**
The word *Amen* assures us that since Jesus has taught us to pray this prayer, the petitions are acceptable to our Father in heaven and will be heard by Him.

25. **Why are you sure that God will hear your prayers?**
God has commanded us to pray and has promised to hear us.

26. **In what word do you express your firm faith?**
In the word *Amen* I affirm my faith in my gracious God. *Amen* means, "Yes, it shall be so." God will indeed answer my prayers.

# Word Study

*to abide:* to remain

*affliction:* misfortune; trouble

*to deliver:* to not allow any evil to harm us

*to deny:* to refuse

*to entice:* to tempt into sin

*to foil:* to bring to nothing; to defeat

*to seduce:* to lead into wrongdoing

*stay:* a support

*Tempter:* the devil

*trespasses:* wrongs; sins

*tribulations:* great suffering and sorrow

# Hymn Stanzas

I need Thy presence ev'ry passing hour;
What but Thy grace can foil the tempter's
    pow'r?
Who like Thyself my guide and stay can be?
Through cloud and sunshine, oh, abide with me.

I fear no foe with Thee at hand to bless;
Ills have no weight, and tears no bitterness.
Where is death's sting? Where, grave, thy victory?
I triumph still if Thou abide with me!

*LW* 490:2, 4

# PRAYER

O God and Father, I am thankful that You are merciful. That is why I beg You to forgive all my sins for Jesus' sake. Make me willing to forgive those who sin against me. Help me resist every temptation the devil sends my way. When I am near death, preserve my faith in Jesus as my Savior and take me to heaven, where I will live surrounded by Your glory. In Jesus' name I pray. Amen.

# WHAT THIS MEANS TO ME

God invites me to pray for both spiritual and material blessings from Him. I know that His spiritual gifts are my most important blessings. In the Lord's Prayer Jesus teaches me to pray for forgiveness of my sins, a forgiving heart, victory over evil temptations, and deliverance from all evils, especially those that will harm my soul.

I pray especially that God will preserve me in true faith and, when He decides to call me home, that He will take me to Himself in heaven.

# UNIT 32  The Sacrament of Holy Baptism

*"Repent and be baptized, every one of you, in the name of Jesus Christ for the forgiveness of your sins."*                    *(Acts 2:38)*

## I. THE NATURE OF BAPTISM

*What is Baptism?*
Baptism is not just plain water, but it is the water included in God's command and combined with God's word.

*Which is that word of God?*
Christ our Lord says in the last chapter of Matthew: "Therefore go and make disciples of all nations, baptizing them in the name of the Father and of the Son and of the Holy Spirit." **[Matt. 28:19]**

## II. THE BLESSINGS OF BAPTISM

*What benefits does Baptism give?*
It works forgiveness of sins, rescues from death and the devil, and gives eternal salvation to all who believe this, as the words and promises of God declare.

*Which are these words and promises of God?*
Christ our Lord says in the last chapter of Mark: "Whoever believes and is baptized will be saved, but whoever does not believe will be condemned." **[Mark 16:16]**

## III. THE POWER OF BAPTISM

*How can water do such great things?*
Certainly not just water, but the word of God in and with the water does these things, along with the faith which trusts this word of God in the water. For without God's word the water is plain water and no Baptism. But

with the word of God it is a Baptism, that is, a life-giving water, rich in grace, and a washing of the new birth in the Holy Spirit, as St. Paul says in Titus, chapter three:

"He saved us through the washing of rebirth and renewal by the Holy Spirit, whom He poured out on us generously through Jesus Christ our Savior, so that, having been justified by His grace, we might become heirs having the hope of eternal life. This is a trustworthy saying." **[Titus 3:5–8]**

## IV. What Baptism Indicates

*What does such baptizing with water indicate?*
It indicates that the Old Adam in us should by daily contrition and repentance be drowned and die with all sins and evil desires, and that a new man should daily emerge and arise to live before God in righteousness and purity forever.

*Where is this written?*
St. Paul writes in Romans chapter six: "We were therefore buried with Him through baptism into death in order that, just as Christ was raised from the dead through the glory of the Father, we too may live a new life." **[Rom. 6:4]**

## Bible Story

### How Jesus Gave the Sacrament of Baptism to His Church　　Matthew 28:16–20

Our Lord Jesus came into the world to save sinners, to make all people God's children. To do this He kept the Law of God perfectly and died on the cross to suffer the punishment of God for all sin. When Jesus rose from the dead, He showed that He had really done everything that was needed to make all sinners the children of God.

The great story of what Jesus has done for all people needs to be proclaimed everywhere. This is the work of the followers of Jesus. When Jesus met His disciples on a mountain in Galilee after His resurrection, He told them, "All authority in heaven and on earth has been given to

Me. Therefore go and make disciples of all nations, baptizing them in the name of the Father and of the Son and of the Holy Spirit; and teaching them to obey everything I have commanded you."

Then Jesus encouraged His disciples in this task by promising them, "Surely I am with you always, to the very end of the age."

## QUESTIONS FOR DISCUSSION

1. **For what purpose did Jesus come into the world?**

2. **What Great Commission did Jesus give to His disciples?**

3. **What two things need to be done to bring people into God's family?**

4. **How does Baptism help the church bring people into the Kingdom?**

# Bible Readings

Therefore go and make disciples of all nations, baptizing them in the name of the Father and of the Son and of the Holy Spirit. Matthew 28:19

No one can enter the kingdom of God unless he is born of water and the Spirit. John 3:5

You are all sons of God through faith in Christ Jesus, for all of you who were baptized into Christ have clothed yourselves with Christ. Galatians 3:26–27

Get up, be baptized and wash your sins away. Acts 22:16

Whoever believes and is baptized will be saved. Mark 16:16

# Bible Teachings

God has commanded that people be baptized. In Baptism water is placed on someone in the name of the Father and of the Son and of the Holy Spirit.

All people, young and old, are to be baptized; Christ, our Lord, commanded His church to baptize all nations. This means little children should also be baptized.

In Baptism we become the children of God and receive the promise of everlasting life. In Baptism God washes away our sins and saves us from death and the devil.

**Note:** Baptismal sponsors assure children that they have been baptized in the way Jesus commanded. They also pray for the children and may help the parents teach God's Word to their godchild, especially if the child's parents should, for some reason, be unable to continue the Christian training of the child.

# QUESTIONS AND ANSWERS

**1. What is a sacrament?**

A sacrament is a sacred act by which forgiveness of sins is imparted through the Gospel and sealed through visible elements.

**2. What two sacraments did God give to His people?**

God gave His people the sacraments of Holy Baptism and the Lord's Supper.

**3. What is Baptism?**

Baptism, a sacrament of the church, is the application of water to a person as God's promises of forgiveness are spoken.

**4. How is Baptism usually given?**

In Baptism water is sprinkled or poured on the head of the person being baptized while these words are spoken: "I baptize you in the name of the Father and of the Son and of the Holy Spirit."

**5. Why should all people, young and old, be baptized?**

All people should be baptized so that by faith in Christ Jesus they might become the children of God.

**6. What has Baptism done for you?**

Baptism has made me a child of God, a member of the church, and an heir of heaven. In Baptism my sins have been washed away.

**7. What did your sponsors promise when you were baptized?**

They promised to pray for me and to help me grow in my Christian faith, especially if my parents are not able to carry out this responsibility. One way that they might do this is to help me receive a Christian education.

# Word Study

*contrition:* sorrow for wrongdoing

*elements:* one of the necessary parts of something; water is an element in Baptism

*regeneration:* spiritual rebirth

*to seal:* to give a sign that something is true

*to signify:* to be a sign of; to mean

*seed:* children; members of a family

*sponsor:* a person who witnesses and answers for an infant at his or her Baptism

# Hymn Stanza

Baptized into Your name most holy,
O Father, Son, and Holy Ghost.
I claim a place, though weak and lowly,
Among Your seed, Your chosen host.
Buried with Christ and dead to sin,
I have Your Spirit now within.

*LW* 224:1

# PRAYER

I thank You, my heavenly Father, that through Baptism You have washed me clean of all my sins and made me Your child. Help me remember throughout my life all that You have done for me in my Baptism. Keep me faithful to You, and bless my parents and sponsors who help me grow as Your child. I pray this in Jesus' name. Amen.

# WHAT THIS MEANS TO ME

I know that when I was baptized my sins were washed away and I became a believing child of God. For this blessing I pray that God would help me live a life of thankful service to Him. Jesus told His disciples to baptize and teach all nations the Gospel. To thank God for my own Baptism, I can support and be active in this work. I pray that the Holy Spirit will enable me to be faithful to my baptismal vow throughout my life.

# UNIT 33

## The Benefits and Meaning of Baptism

*" [Christ cleansed the church] by the washing with water through the Word. " (Ephesians 5:26)*

## BIBLE STORY

### How Paul Was Baptized

Acts 9:1–18

Early in his life Paul the Apostle was an unbeliever. He hated Jesus and those who followed Him. Nothing gave Paul, then called Saul, greater pleasure than to hunt down Christians, drag them to jail, and have them killed. When he heard that there were Christians in Damascus, Saul decided to go there to arrest them.

He did not get to carry out his plan. Near Damascus a light from heaven suddenly struck him and knocked him from his horse. Jesus Himself called, "Saul, Saul, why are you persecuting Me?"

"Who are You, Lord?" Saul cried.

"I am Jesus, whom you are persecuting," Jesus answered.

"Lord, what do You want me to do?" asked Saul, trembling and astonished.

"Get up and go into the city," Jesus replied, "and you will be told what to do."

Blind and afraid, Saul was led by his companions into Damascus. For three days he sat in a room in Judas's home on Straight Street without eating or drinking. Did he think about all the terrible things he had done against the Lord Jesus and His followers? If so, how depressed he must have become! Could his wicked deeds ever be forgiven?

Three days later a Christian who lived in Damascus, Ananias, came to visit Saul. He told Saul, "The Lord Jesus, who spoke to you on the road, sent me to you so that you may see again and be filled with the Holy Spirit." Immediately Saul was able to see. He got up, was baptized, and began eating again. In years to come the Lord made him a great apostle in the kingdom of the Lord Jesus Christ. Then he became known as Paul.

## QUESTIONS FOR DISCUSSION

1. **Describe some of the sins Paul committed against Jesus.**
2. **Why did Paul stop hunting Christians?**
3. **How were Paul's sins washed away?**
4. **What does your Baptism mean to you?**

## BIBLE READINGS

Go and make disciples of all nations, baptizing them in the name of the Father and of the Son and of the Holy Spirit. Matthew 28:19

Christ loved the church and gave Himself up for her to make her holy, cleansing her by the washing with water through the word. Ephesians 5:25–26

Repent and be baptized, every one of you, in the name of Jesus Christ for the forgiveness of your sins. Acts 2:38

You are all sons of God through faith in Christ Jesus, for all of you who were baptized into Christ have clothed yourselves with Christ. Galatians 3:26–27

If anyone is in Christ, he is a new creation. 2 Corinthians 5:17

## "Repent and be Baptized."

## BIBLE TEACHINGS

By His holy life and by His innocent suffering and death, Christ earned forgiveness of sins for everyone. The Sacrament of Holy Baptism makes this forgiveness our own. Baptism has this wonderful power because water is used in the name of the Father and of the Son and of the Holy Spirit.

The Holy Spirit works through Baptism and makes this sacrament a heavenly washing. Through Baptism all our sins are washed away, and we become members of God's family.

The blessings of Baptism become our own through faith, as Jesus said, "Whoever believes and is baptized will be saved" (Mark 16:16). The Holy Spirit gives us this faith in our Baptism.

# QUESTIONS AND ANSWERS

**1. What great blessings do we receive through Baptism?**

We receive forgiveness of sins, life, and salvation.

**2. In what words does Jesus promise us these blessings?**

He says, "Whoever believes and is baptized will be saved" (Mark 16:16).

**3. How can the water of Baptism give such great blessings?**

It is not just the water that gives such great blessings, but the water combined with God's Word in the Sacrament produces the blessing of faith.

**4. What vow did you make through your sponsors at the time of your Baptism?**

At my Baptism I renounced the devil and all his works and all his ways. I also stated that I believe in God the Father, God the Son, and God the Holy Spirit, and that I believe that Jesus is my Savior. With the help of God, I will lead a Christian life.

**5. How often should you renew your baptismal vow?**

I should renew my baptismal vow every day.

**6. Is it necessary to be baptized again to be made clean?**

No. Even though we sin, God remains faithful to His promise of forgiveness given in Baptism.

**7. Why can you always find comfort and joy in the fact that you have been baptized?**

In my Baptism I was born again and made a child of God.

# WORD STUDY

*to persecute:* to harass or cause someone to suffer for a belief

*remission:* forgiveness

*sacrament:* a sacred act instituted by God in which He

joins His Word of forgiveness through Jesus to a visible element (water or bread and wine) to bring His forgiveness of sins to people

*to sanctify:* to make holy

*vow:* a solemn promise

*"washing with water through the word"* Holy Baptism

# HYMN STANZA

All who believe and are baptized
Shall see the Lord's salvation;
Baptized into the death of Christ,
They are a new creation;
Through Christ's redemption they will stand
Among the glorious heav'nly band
Of ev'ry tribe and nation.

*LW* 225:1

# PRAYER

Dear Father in heaven, I thank You that through my Baptism You have forgiven all my sins and made me Your child. Keep me in Your family. By Your Holy Spirit's power, help me live as Your child and give me everlasting life as You have promised. I pray this through Jesus Christ, my Lord. Amen.

# WHAT THIS MEANS TO ME

In my Baptism I became a member of God's family. To remain God's child, I pray that God would give me a firm faith that continues to believe in Jesus, who earned the forgiveness I received in my Baptism. My Baptism is not a magic ticket to heaven. Jesus reminds me of this when He says, "Whoever believes and is baptized will be saved, but whoever does not believe will be condemned" (Mark 16:16).

# UNIT 34    The Authority to Forgive Sins

*"Repent and believe the good news."* (Mark 1:15)

## THE OFFICE OF THE KEYS

*What is the Office of the Keys?*
The Office of the Keys is that special authority which Christ has given to His church on earth to forgive the sins of repentant sinners, but to withhold forgiveness from the unrepentant as long as they do not repent.

*Where is this written?*
This is what St. John the Evangelist writes in chapter twenty: The Lord Jesus breathed on His disciples and said, "Receive the Holy Spirit. If you forgive anyone his sins, they are forgiven; if you do not forgive them, they are not forgiven." **[John 20:22–23]**

*What do you believe according to these words?*
I believe that when the called ministers of Christ deal with us by His divine command, in particular when they exclude openly unrepentant sinners from the Christian congregation and absolve those who repent of their sins and want to do better, this is just as valid and certain, even in heaven, as if Christ our dear Lord dealt with us Himself.

# CONFESSION AND ABSOLUTION

*What is Confession?*
Confession has two parts.

First that we confess our sins, and second, that we receive absolution, that is, forgiveness, from the pastor as from God Himself, not doubting, but firmly believing that by it our sins are forgiven before God in heaven.

*What sins should we confess?*
Before God we should plead guilty of all sins, even those we are not aware of, as we do in the Lord's Prayer; but before the pastor we should confess only those sins which we know and feel in our hearts.

*Which are these?*
Consider your place in life according to the Ten Commandments: Are you a father, mother, son, daughter, husband, wife, or worker? Have you been disobedient, unfaithful, or lazy? Have you been hot-tempered, rude, or quarrelsome? Have you hurt someone by your words or deeds? Have you stolen, been negligent, wasted anything, or done any harm?

# Bible Story

### *Nathan and David*        2 Samuel 12:1–13

David was a great king and a man after God's own heart. Yet he was not perfect; he was not without sin. At one time he so completely forgot God that he had an affair with Uriah's wife and then had Uriah murdered. For some time David was not sorry for his sins, and God was very angry with him. Finally, God sent His prophet Nathan to show David his sins.

Nathan told David this story: "There were two men living next door to each other. The one was very rich and the other very poor. The rich man had many sheep and cattle; but the poor man had nothing but one little lamb. He loved it so much that he let it drink from his own cup and eat some of the family food. The little lamb was the beloved pet of the poor man and his children.

"One day the rich man had a visitor. Instead of taking a lamb from his own big flock, the rich man took the poor man's only lamb, had it killed, and served it to his guests."

When Nathan stopped, King David became angry and shouted, "As surely as there is a God, the man who did this cruel thing will be put to death!"

"You are the man!" Nathan answered. "You did this when you killed Uriah and married his wife."

Now David was truly sorry for his sins. He said, "I have sinned against the Lord."

Nathan then comforted him by saying, "The Lord has put away your sin; you shall not die."

## QUESTIONS FOR DISCUSSION

1. **Can a child of God commit terrible sins?**

2. **How did David make his sins even worse?**

3. **Describe how Nathan showed David the greatness of his sins.**

4. **In which words did David show that he was truly sorry?**

5. **Once David had confessed his sin, what message could and did Nathan announce to him?**

## BIBLE READINGS

If we claim to be without sin, we deceive ourselves and the truth is not in us. If we confess our sins, He is faithful and just and will forgive us our sins and purify us from all unrighteousness. 1 John 1:8–9

[Jesus] breathed on [His disciples] and said, "Receive the Holy Spirit. If you forgive anyone his sins, they are forgiven; if you do not forgive them, they are not forgiven. John 20:22–23

What I have forgiven—if there was anything to forgive—I have forgiven in the sight of Christ for your sake. 2 Corinthians 2:10

I will give you the keys of the kingdom of heaven. Matthew 16:19

# Bible Teachings

All people, even Christians, are sinners. That is why, in almost every church service, the people confess their sins and ask God for forgiveness. The pastor then announces to the congregation that their sins are forgiven in the name of God. We call this announcement of forgiveness the absolution.

God has given to *all* believers the power to forgive sins. They should use it. Publicly, Christian people use this power through their pastor, whom they have called for this purpose.

Only those people who are penitent, that is, who are truly sorry for their sins and believe in Jesus as their Savior, will have their sins forgiven.

The power to forgive sins is called the Office of the Keys because heaven is opened to sinners when their sins are forgiven, or it is closed when their sins are not forgiven.

# Questions and Answers

1. **How do we obtain the forgiveness that God has promised?**
   We obtain forgiveness when we confess our sins to God and ask Him for forgiveness.

2. **For whose sake does God forgive the sins we confess?**
   God forgives our sins for the sake of Jesus.

3. **Why is God willing to pardon us for Jesus' sake?**
   Jesus lived a perfect life for us, suffered the punishment for sin that we should have suffered, and died for us. Because His Son, Jesus, has done all this for us, God graciously forgives our sin.

4. **Where is this message of forgiveness explained?**
   This message of forgiveness, the Gospel, is explained in the Bible.

5. **To whom has God entrusted the power to proclaim the forgiveness of sins?**
   God has entrusted the proclamation of the Gospel to

every Christian and every Christian congregation.

**6. How does the Christian congregation use this power?**

The congregation calls a pastor to publicly announce the absolution, or forgiveness of sins, on its behalf.

**7. Is the absolution spoken by the pastor honored by God also?**

Yes. It is as valid and certain with God in heaven as if Christ, our dear Lord, had announced forgiveness to us Himself.

**8. Who receives the benefit of absolution?**

All penitent sinners receive the benefit of absolution.

**9. Who are penitent sinners?**

Penitent sinners are all those who are sorry for their sins and believe in Jesus as their Savior.

**10. Why is the power to forgive sins called The Office of the Keys?**

Like a key that can open or lock a door, so the authority to announce forgiveness of sins or to withhold this forgiveness opens heaven to penitent sinners or locks heaven to unrepentant sinners.

**11. What are the words of absolution that are spoken by the pastor?**

The words of absolution are as follows: Upon this your confession, I, by virtue of my office as a called and ordained servant of the Word, announce the grace of God to all of you, and in the stead and by the command of my Lord Jesus Christ, I forgive you all your sins in the name of the Father and of the Son and of the Holy Spirit.

# WORD STUDY

*absolution:* announcement of freedom from the guilt of sin

*contrite:* sorry for wrongdoing

*"guard our race":* protect the human race

*impenitent:* not sorry for wrongdoing

*peculiar:* special; belonging to

*to purge:* to make clean

*to remit:* to forgive; to pardon

*to retain:* to keep; to hold back; not to forgive

*slothful:* lazy

*valid:* true

# HYMN STANZAS

The words which absolution give
Are His who died that we might live;
The minister whom Christ has sent
Is but His humble instrument.

All praise to You, O Christ, shall be
For absolution full and free,
In which You show Your richest grace;
From false indulgence guard our race.

*LW* 235:5, 7

# PRAYER

God, be merciful to me, a sinner. Cleanse me, and I will be clean; wash me, and I will be whiter than snow. Create in me a pure heart. Do not cast me away from Your presence or take Your Holy Spirit from me. Restore to me the joy of Your salvation, and sustain a willing spirit in me. Hear me for the sake of Jesus, who loved me and gave Himself for me. Amen.

# WHAT THIS MEANS TO ME

Since my unforgiven sins separate me from God, I need to humbly repent of them and to ask God to forgive them. I can do this privately each day. Publicly, I can confess my sins together with my fellow believers in our worship services. When I confess my sins, firmly believing in Jesus who earned my forgiveness, the doors of heaven will be unlocked so that I may enter.

*UNIT 35* THE LORD'S SUPPER

*"This is My body. . . . This is My blood."*
*(Mark 14: 22, 24)*

# I. THE NATURE
## OF THE SACRAMENT OF THE ALTAR

*What is the Sacrament of the Altar?*
It is the true body and blood of our Lord Jesus Christ
under the bread and wine, instituted by Christ Himself for
us Christians to eat and to drink.

*Where is this written?*
The holy Evangelists Matthew, Mark, Luke, and St. Paul
write:

Our Lord Jesus Christ, on the night when He was
betrayed, took bread, and when He had given thanks, He
broke it and gave it to the disciples and said: "Take, eat;
this is My body, which is given for you. This do in
remembrance of Me."

In the same way also He took the cup after supper, and
when He had given thanks, He gave it to them, saying,
"Drink of it, all of you; this cup is the new testament in
My blood, which is shed for you for the forgiveness of
sins. This do, as often as you drink it, in remembrance of
Me."

# II. THE BENEFIT
## OF THE SACRAMENT OF THE ALTAR

*What is the benefit of this eating and drinking?*
These words, "Given and shed for you for the forgiveness of
sins," show us that in the Sacrament forgiveness of sins, life,
and salvation are given us through these words. For where
there is forgiveness of sins, there is also life and salvation.

# III. The Power
## of the Sacrament of the Altar

*How can bodily eating and drinking do such great things?*
Certainly not just the eating and drinking do these
things, but the words written here: "Given and shed for
you for the forgiveness of sins." These words, along with
the bodily eating and drinking, are the main thing in the
Sacrament. Whoever believes these words has exactly
what they say: "forgiveness of sins."

# IV. How to Receive
## This Sacrament Worthily

*Who receives this sacrament worthily?*
Fasting and bodily preparation are certainly fine outward
training. But that person is truly worthy and well-pre-
pared who has faith in these words: "Given and shed for
you for the forgiveness of sins."

But anyone who does not believe these words or doubts
them is unworthy and unprepared, for the words "for
you" require all hearts to believe.

## Bible Story

### *How the Lord's Supper Was First Celebrated*

Mark 14:12–24

On the Thursday evening after Palm Sunday Jesus
sent Peter and John into Jerusalem to prepare the
Passover meal for Him and His 12 disciples. "Where
shall we prepare it?" they asked.

Jesus said, "Go into the city. You will meet a man
carrying a pitcher of water. Follow him. He will lead you
to a house. The owner of that house will let you have a
large upstairs room for our meal."

They followed Jesus' directions and found everything as He had described it. When everything was ready,
Jesus and the Twelve gathered around the table. Lovingly

Jesus said to them, "I have longed to eat this Passover with you before I suffer and die."

At the end of the Passover meal, Jesus took bread. After He had given thanks, He broke the bread in pieces and gave pieces to each of His disciples. While He did this He said, "Take, eat; *this is My body*, which is given for you. Eat this to remember Me."

Then He took the cup of wine, gave thanks, and gave it to them to drink. "Drink of it;" He said, "this is the new testament in *My blood*, which is shed for you for the forgiveness of sins. Drink this often to remember Me."

## QUESTIONS FOR DISCUSSION

1. **When did Jesus celebrate the Passover with His disciples?**

2. **Where was this meal eaten?**

3. **After the regular meal was completed, what special gift did Jesus give to His disciples and the church?**

4. **What did Jesus say about the bread and the wine that He served?**

# BIBLE READINGS

Take it; this is My body. Mark 14:22

This is My blood of the covenant, which is poured out for many. Mark 14:24

Is not the cup of thanksgiving for which we give thanks a participation in the blood of Christ? And is not the bread that we break a participation in the body of Christ? 1 Corinthians 10:16

Whenever you eat this bread and drink this cup, you proclaim the Lord's death until He comes. 1 Corinthians 11:26

# BIBLE TEACHINGS

The Sacrament of the Altar is also called the Lord's Supper because it was instituted by our Lord during the evening Passover meal on a day we now call Maundy Thursday.

In this Holy Supper Christ gives His true body and blood to all who eat the bread and drink the wine with faith.

We cannot understand how it is possible to receive bread and wine as well as His body and blood in this sacrament, but we believe we receive all of these elements because Christ said, when He gave the bread, *"This is My body,"* and when He gave the wine He said, *"This is My blood."* What Christ says is true; with God nothing is impossible.

# QUESTIONS AND ANSWERS

1. **What sacrament did Jesus give to His church to strengthen the spiritual life begun in Baptism?**
   Jesus gave the Sacrament of the Altar, or Holy Communion, to strengthen the spiritual life begun in Baptism.

2. **What is Holy Communion?**
   Holy Communion is the receiving of the body and blood of Christ in, with, and under the bread and wine. In Holy Communion the believer receives forgiveness of sins.

3. **What earthly elements do we receive in the Sacrament of the Altar?**
Those who participate in the Lord's Supper receive bread and wine.

4. **What spiritual gifts do those who participate in the Sacrament receive together with the bread and the wine in the Sacrament of the Altar?**
Participants in the Sacrament receive Christ's body and blood together with the bread and the wine.

5. **Do you believe, then, that the body and blood of Christ are really present in the Sacrament?**
Yes, I believe it.

6. **What causes you to believe this?**
The words of Christ, "This is My body," and "This is My blood," assure me that I receive Christ's body when I eat the bread and I receive Christ's blood when I drink the wine.

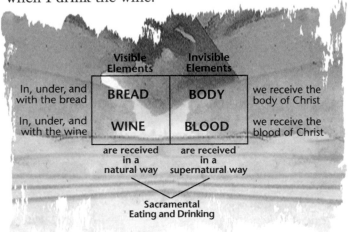

7. **What do you remember when you eat His body and drink His blood?**
I remember that through His suffering, death, and resurrection I receive forgiveness of my sins; Jesus said, "Do this in remembrance of Me" (Luke 22:19).

8. **Why do Christians want to go to the Sacrament?**
Christians, myself included, want to receive the Sacrament because in it they receive forgiveness of sins.

In this Sacrament I am strengthened in my belief that Christ, out of great love, died for my sin and I am empowered to love God and my neighbor.

9. **How often do you participate in this Sacrament?**
I want to participate in the Sacrament frequently because God has promised to bless me through this Sacrament. I also need to participate frequently because of the pardon, peace, and strength it brings to me.

10. **How often should you receive the Lord's Supper?**
I want to receive it regularly and frequently since I need this food and drink to nourish my soul, just as I need food and drink to nourish my body.

## WORD STUDY

*beneficial:* helpful

*communion:* joining together

*evangelist:* one of the writers of the life and words of Christ

*to fast:* to go without food for a period of time

*to induce:* to cause

*to institute:* to establish; to begin; Christ instituted the Sacrament of the Altar

*naught:* nothing

*testament:* will; agreement; promise; covenant

# Hymn Stanza

I eat this bread, I drink this cup,
Your promise firm believing;
In truth Your body and Your blood
My lips are here receiving.
Your Word remains forever true;
All things are possible for You;
Your searching love has found me.

*LW 246:3*

# Prayer

We thank You, Lord Jesus, for Your Holy Supper, which You have prepared for Your children on earth. Preserve this blessed Sacrament among us until the end of days. Amen.

# What This Means to Me

Jesus has told me that in the Lord's Supper I receive His true body and blood. Even though I cannot understand how His body and blood can be received with the bread and wine, I believe Jesus' words because His Word is always true. By God's grace I know that my sins are forgiven through Jesus. For the strengthening of my faith, I will celebrate this Sacrament often, as God's Word has encouraged me to do (Matthew 11:28).

# UNIT 36 — The Benefit of the Lord's Supper

*"Whoever comes to Me I will never drive away."* (John 6:37)

## BIBLE STORY

### A Father Forgives His Prodigal Son   Luke 15:11–32

A man had two sons. He loved them both and made their home as happy and pleasant as he could. The younger son, however, did not like it at home. One day he came to his father and said, "Father, give me my share of my inheritance." So the father gave him his share.

Not long after this the younger son took all he had

263

and left home. He went to a faraway country and wasted his inheritance by wild and wicked living. As long as he had money, he had friends.

It did not take him very long to spend everything. When his money was gone, his friends deserted him. To keep himself alive, he worked for a farmer feeding pigs. He became so desperate he longed to eat the pigs' food, but no one offered him anything to eat. When he came to his senses, he remembered how wonderful his home was. "My father's servants have bread to spare," he said, "and here I am starving!" He began to realize how foolish and wicked he had been to leave home.

Finally he decided to go back to his father. After long and weary days of walking, he finally came near his home.

His father had been watching for him every day. When he saw his son walking on the road, he ran out to meet him. With a joyful heart he took his son into his arms and hugged him.

"Father, I have sinned against God and you," the son cried. "I don't deserve to be called your son anymore."

The father didn't want to hear this. He told his servants to bring the best clothes for his son and then to prepare a big feast. "My son was dead," he said, "but now he's alive; he was lost, but now he is found."

Jesus told this parable to explain how much God loves sinners and how gladly He will forgive their sins.

## QUESTIONS FOR DISCUSSION

1. **What did the younger son ask his father to give him?**

2. **What did he do with his gift?**

3. **What happened to him when his money was gone?**

4. **How did the father treat the son when he came home?**

5. **What did Jesus teach us about God in this parable?**

# BIBLE READINGS

In [Christ] we have redemption through His blood, the forgiveness of sins, in accordance with the riches of God's grace. Ephesians 1:7

Come to Me, all you who are weary and burdened, and I will give you rest. Matthew 11:28

This is My body given for you. Luke 22:19

This is My blood of the covenant, which is poured out for many for the forgiveness of sins. Matthew 26:28

A man ought to examine himself before he eats of the bread and drinks of the cup. For anyone who eats and drinks without recognizing the body of the Lord eats and drinks judgment on himself. 1 Corinthians 11:28–29

# BIBLE TEACHINGS

With His suffering and death, Christ has redeemed us and earned for us the forgiveness of all our sins. Now He graciously invites all sinners to come to Him in true faith and receive forgiveness.

In the Lord's Supper our Savior offers and gives His forgiveness to believers in a special way. He does this by sealing this gift to believers with His body and His blood, making believers personally sure that their sins are forgiven.

It is, therefore, very important for all who participate in the Sacrament of the Altar to examine themselves concerning their faith in the promises of Jesus. For this reason the church instructs people about the Sacrament and prepares them to examine themselves before they receive the Sacrament.

# QUESTIONS AND ANSWERS

**1. What blessings does the Sacrament of the Altar give to believers?**

The Sacrament of the Altar gives forgiveness of sins, life, and salvation.

**2. Which words in the Sacrament contain the promise of this blessing?**

Jesus' words "given and shed for you for the forgiveness of sins" bring this promise to God's people.

**3. What special seal does Christ attach to the words in the Sacrament?**

He attaches His body and blood to these words as His special seal.

**4. Why can each individual communicant be sure that Jesus died for him or her?**

In the Sacrament Jesus gives each person the very body and blood with which He earned forgiveness for all on the cross.

**5. May a person who is weak in faith go to the Lord's Supper?**

Yes, indeed. The Lord's Supper strengthens everyone's faith.

**6. How will the Lord's Supper help us in our relationship to God?**

The Lord's Supper reminds those who participate of God's kindness to them. It also encourages them to be thankful for His blessings.

**7. How will the Lord's Supper help us in our relationship to other people?**

The Lord's Supper helps us remember that we who commune at the same altar are one in Christ, and it helps us love and better serve others.

**8. Why do you want to receive Holy Communion frequently?**

I need to have my faith strengthened, my love increased, and my soul nurtured until I am given life everlasting.

9. **Why is it important for you to be instructed in the Christian religion before you receive Holy Communion?**
I need to understand and appreciate the blessings that God intends for me in Holy Communion.

10. **How may you properly prepare yourself for the right reception of the Lord's Supper?**
I can prepare myself for participation in the Sacrament of the Altar by using the following questions to examine myself:

> † Am I sorry that I have sinned against God?
>
> † Do I believe that Jesus died for my sins and that He gives me His body and blood in the Sacrament of the Altar?
>
> † Do I plan, with God's help, to change the sinful parts of my life?

I can also use the Christian Questions with Their Answers to prepare for receiving the Sacrament of the Altar.

## WORD STUDY

*assurance:* certainty; sureness

*communicant:* a person who partakes of Holy Communion

*to discern:* to see; to recognize the importance of

*to nurture:* to nourish; to feed

*prodigal:* wasteful; foolish in spending money or using possessions

*to seal:* to make sure

# Hymn Stanza

Sent forth by God's blessing,
Our true faith confessing,
The people of God from His dwelling take
    leave.
The supper is ended.
Oh, now be extended
The fruits of this service in all who believe.
The seed of His teaching,
Receptive souls reaching,
Shall blossom in action for God and for all.
His grace did invite us,
His love shall unite us
To work for God's kingdom and answer His
    call.

*LW* 247**:1

## Prayer

Dear Savior, I thank You that through Your body and blood in the Sacrament of the Altar believers are made sure of the forgiveness of their sins. Bless all who are guests at Your table with true faith in Your Word and promises. Keep me faithful throughout my life and give me the crown of life in heaven. Amen.

## What This Means to Me

In the Lord's Supper Jesus graciously offers me the wonderful gift of forgiveness in a special way. His body and His blood, received with the bread and wine, and joined with His forgiving Word, make me sure that my sins are forgiven. When I celebrate the Sacrament with sorrow for my sins and faith in Jesus, who earned forgiveness for me, I will have and hold the greatest of all blessings—peace through the pardoning of my sins.

** Sent Forth by God's Blessing. Text by Omer Westendorf copyright © 1994, World Library Publications www.wlpmusic.com. All rights reserved. Used by permission.

*On his return from Worms, Luther was kidnapped by friends and taken to the Wartburg, where he hid for almost a year.*

# The Life of Martin Luther (1483–1546)

Martin Luther was born in the town of Eisleben, Germany, on November 10, 1483. He was the son of a hard-working miner, Hans Luther, and his wife, Margaret. Young Martin grew up in a home where the parents prayed faithfully to the saints and taught their children to do likewise. His father and mother loved their children dearly, but they were also very strict with them.

## LUTHER AT SCHOOL

When Martin was five years old, he went to school in Mansfeld, where his parents had moved. In this school he studied the Ten Commandments, the Apostles' Creed, the Lord's Prayer, church music, Latin, and mathematics. The sad part of the instruction was that Martin and his fellow pupils learned little about the *love* of God. They learned to know Jesus not as the friend of sinners, but as the judge of those who sinned. They feared Jesus but did not love Him.

Martin learned rapidly, for he was a bright boy who studied diligently. When he became 14 he was admitted to the Latin High School at Magdeburg, 60 miles from his home. Here, for the first time, Luther saw a Bible. The next year his father transferred him to a school in Eisenach. Here a rich and pious woman, Mrs. Ursula Cotta, took a special liking to him. At one time, when a group of boys was singing outside her home, she invited

Martin in and offered him free lodging. He readily accepted. He received free meals in another home where he taught a young child of the family. Luther was now able to devote more time to his studies. In addition, since the Cotta family was a cultured family, he was exposed to music, art, and conversation with interesting visitors. He soon began to appreciate music and art, and he developed his remarkable musical talent.

## LUTHER AT THE UNIVERSITY

By the time Martin Luther was prepared to enter the university, his father had become a prosperous man who could afford to send Martin to college. Recognizing his son's gifts, Hans Luther wanted his son to become a lawyer, so he sent him to the University of Erfurt. Here again Martin studied diligently, spending much time in the library. At the age of 21 he was awarded the Master of Arts degree. Now he was able to teach.

To please his father, Martin remained at the university to study law, but he soon lost interest in that subject. More and more he studied religion and worried over his sinful condition. No matter how hard he tried to please God, he could not find peace for his soul.

## LUTHER AS A MONK

One day a close friend of his died suddenly. Luther was so shaken by this death that he became fearful and deeply disturbed. He asked himself, "What will happen to me in eternity?" A little later, while returning to Erfurt from a visit to his parents, he was caught in a violent thunderstorm. Almost frantic with fear, young Luther promised St. Anne that he would become a monk.

When he returned to the university, Martin sold his books, said farewell to his friends, and, deaf to their pleadings, entered the Augustinian monastery at Erfurt. "Now," he said, "I will certainly be able to lead a far more God-pleasing life than I did at the university." In the Black Cloister, as the monastery was called because of the black robes the monks wore, Brother Martin was given a small, unheated cell as his room. It was only 7 feet wide and 10 feet long; it contained a table, a chair, a straw bed, and a window.

In the monastery Luther continued his study of the Bible. Dressed in the black robe and small cap that was to be worn day and night, he faithfully engaged in the daily religious exercises prescribed by the Augustinian Order. He also spent time trudging through the streets of the city, a sack on his back, as was the custom, begging for bread, butter, eggs, and whatever else he could get for the monastery. In addition, he swept the chapel, cleaned the rooms, rang the bells, and performed similar work. Back in his cell, he diligently studied religion and philosophy, and he prayed to the saints, eagerly striving to earn his way to heaven through his own good works. More than ever, he was searching for peace of soul; but he could not find rest. One thought was constantly on his mind. It made him very unhappy. "I am a sinner," he said to himself, "and my sins move God to anger." He was sure he could never do enough good works to please God. As time went on, however, and as he continued to study the Bible, he made the marvelous discovery that salvation is a free gift from God through the Savior, Jesus Christ.

## LUTHER AS PRIEST, TEACHER, AND PREACHER

In the spring of 1507, Luther, now 23, became a priest. His superiors thought so highly of him that he was asked to teach at the University of Erfurt and the newly founded University of Wittenberg. He soon became known as a great teacher of the Bible. Students came in great numbers to listen to his lectures.

His work as teacher was interrupted, however, by a request from his Father Superior. Dr. Staupitz asked him to go to Rome, where the Pope lived, to help settle a dispute in the Augustinian Order. He and a companion set out on foot to travel to Rome. The journey was long and difficult; the two travelers spent their nights in monasteries along the way. When they finally saw the city before them, Luther fell on his knees and cried out, "Hail, holy city of Rome!" As he visited churches in the city, however, he was greatly disappointed by the sinful life he saw and the negligent manner in which church services were conducted.

After his return five months later, Luther resumed his teaching at the University of Wittenberg. In the fall of 1512, he had earned the title Doctor of Divinity. Besides teaching at the university, he also began to preach in the large Castle Church. Never before had the people heard the Word of God proclaimed so richly and so eloquently. They flocked in ever-increasing numbers to hear him. In his sermons Luther warned his hearers against trying to *earn* salvation by good works and pleaded with them to accept God's offer of free salvation in Jesus.

## LUTHER POSTS NINETY-FIVE THESES AGAINST INDULGENCES

Common in those days was the practice of selling indulgences for money. People who purchased these indulgences were promised freedom from punishment of their sins on earth and in purgatory. John Tetzel, an indulgence salesman, came to a town near Wittenberg. He urged people to buy forgiveness for all past, present, and future sins. Some of Luther's church members purchased these worthless indulgence letters. Because they owned indulgences, they boldly refused to repent of their sins. Their impenitence roused Luther to action. He refused to give such members Absolution and the Sacrament of the Altar unless they repented of their sins. Deeply disturbed by the attitude of the people, Luther preached many sermons on repentance. Finally he wrote Ninety-five Theses, or sentences, in which he condemned the sale of indulgences. On October 31, 1517, he posted these Ninety-five Theses on the university bulletin board, the door of the Castle Church. In one of his theses he stated, "Every Christian who truly repents has full forgiveness, even without letters of pardon."

Thousands of people, both in high places and low, were glad that Luther had spoken out against this practice of the church.

## LUTHER AT WORMS

When Pope Leo X in Rome heard of what Luther had done and of the reaction to his theses in Germany, he was furious and threatened Luther with excommunication if he did not recant within 60 days. Luther remained firm, however, because he felt that he was right and that he had acted for the glory of God. In 1521 Luther was ordered to appear before the Diet of Worms for trial. At this convention the highest officials of the church and of the governments were present. Here again Luther was asked to recant his statements and writings. Not one opponent could bring forward a word from the Bible to show that Luther was mistaken. Luther, therefore, refused to change anything that he had said or written.

# LUTHER AT THE WARTBURG

At the end of the proceedings at Worms Emperor Charles V declared that Luther was an outlaw; anyone could kill him without fear of punishment. Although his life was in great danger, Luther began his return journey to Wittenberg. While he and his party were riding through a forest, a band of masked men rushed upon them, took him prisoner, and rode with him to a castle, the Wartburg. At midnight the heavy drawbridge was lowered, and Luther disappeared behind the massive castle walls. Only a few people knew where Luther was, and they guarded their secret well. Some people thought that Luther was dead. What they did not know was that some of his friends had secretly kidnapped him and had brought him to this safe place.

Meanwhile Luther, disguised as a knight, lived at the Wartburg and translated the New Testament into the German language so that the common people might easily read and understand the Word of God. Since printing with movable type had been invented shortly before this time by Johann Gutenburg, copies of Luther's writings were soon in the hands of many people. His translation of the New Testament appeared in September 1522.

Luther remained in seclusion at the Wartburg for almost a year. Then he returned to Wittenberg. He preached eight powerful sermons to clear away certain errors that had crept into the church while he was gone. In his sermons he tried to show the people what the new way of life, lived under the Gospel, was really like. He warned them against using force in their struggle against the Pope and his followers. Their sole weapon, he said, was only to be the powerful Word of God. From Wittenberg Luther went to a number of towns and communities, everywhere counseling to use their liberty from papal tyranny for only one purpose—to become better Christians.

Luther lived in constant danger of being arrested and killed. Although his friends were worried, no one ever touched him. That he remained alive seems like a miracle.

# LUTHER AT HOME

On June 13, 1525, Luther married Katherina von Bora, a former nun. The wedding ceremony took place in the Black Cloister in Wittenberg, a part of which had been changed into living quarters for Luther. God blessed this marriage with three boys and three girls. Luther loved home life. He took time to play with his children, to make music with them, and to write letters to them when he was away from home. He was also interested in gardening and in the problems of running a household. He had many visitors. Although Luther was a man of modest means, he was very generous. His kindness and liberality to others sometimes worried his wife, especially since Luther was extremely hospitable and would freely give shelter, food, and even money to the unfortunate.

# LUTHER WRITES THE CATECHISM
## AND A HYMNBOOK

Knowing that Christian faith must be based on Christian knowledge, Luther organized Christian schools. To help parents, pastors, and teachers instruct children in the Christian faith, he wrote the Small Catechism in 1529. Next to the Bible, it is the most widely used book in the Lutheran church. This book is used in churches and schools yet today. Luther wrote a number of beautiful hymns, published the first Protestant hymnbook in 1524, and encouraged other able writers and composers to write hymn texts and tunes for use in worship. He helped write the Augsburg Confession, published in 1530. He completed the translation of the Old Testament in 1534. Though hampered by ill health, he continued to be active, both among the people and in the quiet of his study. His writings fill many volumes. He continued to work hard until the day before he died.

## LUTHER'S LAST DAYS

On January 23, 1546, at the urgent invitation of the princes of Mansfeld, Luther left Wittenberg for Eisleben. Since he did not feel well enough to make the trip alone, he took his two sons Martin and Paul with him. The weather was snowy and the roads were hard to travel. It took five days to travel the 80 miles to Eisleben. Luther went only because this was to be a mission of loving serv-

ice. He had been invited to
help re-establish peace in a
family torn by bitter strife.
It was a trying experience
for him. After 20 days of
patient counseling, however, he brought about a rec-
onciliation between the two
men. His ailing body,
though, was completely
exhausted. On February 17,
in the evening, he was
taken to his room to rest;
near him were his sons and
three close friends. Luther
knew that his end was
approaching. In fervent
words of prayer he committed his soul to his heavenly
Father. He was asked
whether he was ready to die
in the name of the Lord

Jesus Christ, whose doctrine he had preached. He
answered with a distinct Yes. He now dropped into a fit-
ful sleep. At about 2 A.M. the angels of God carried his
soul to heaven, safe with his Savior, the Lord Jesus
Christ.

Luther died on February 18, 1546. His body was
taken to Wittenberg, where a funeral service was held on
February 22. He was buried in the Castle Church in a
grave directly in front of the pulpit. Luther is dead, but
his works live after him. The reformation of the church,
which he began, has been continued in all parts of the
world. Jesus, the King of Grace, whom Luther proclaimed, lives in the hearts of millions of believers. After
almost 500 years, Luther is still honored as the great
teacher of the Lutheran Church and of all Protestantism.

"Remember your leaders, who spoke the word of
God to you. Consider the outcome of their way of life
and imitate their faith" (Hebrews 13:7).

For being near, for parents dear,
for food and drink—
I thank You, Lord.

# Children's Prayers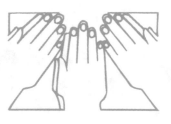

## *MORNING*

Father, we thank You for the night,
And for the pleasant morning light;
For health and friends and loving care,
And all that makes this world so fair.

Help us do the things we should,
To be to others kind and good;
In all we do, at work and play,
To grow more loving ev'ry day. Amen.

*Rebecca Weston, ca. 1890, alt.*

Jesus, tender Shepherd,
Hear me while I pray;
Guide and keep me safely
Through the coming day. Amen.

Father, lead me, day by day,
Always in Your loving way.
Show me praises I might bring;
Teach me to delight my King. Amen.

Help me, Lord, this day to be
Your own dear child, saved and free;
Lead me, Savior, by Your hand
'Til I reach the heavenly land. Amen.

## EVENING

Now I lay me down to sleep,
I pray You, Lord, my soul to keep;
If I should die before I wake,
I pray, O Lord, my soul You'd take;
All this I ask for Jesus' sake. Amen.

Jesus, tender Shepherd, hear me;
Bless Your little lamb tonight.
Through the darkness, Lord, be near me;
Keep me safe till morning light. Amen.

*Mary L. Duncan, 1814–40, alt.*

All this day Your hand has led me,
And I thank You for Your care.
You have clothed me, warmed and fed me;
Listen to my evening prayer. Amen.

Lord Jesus, since You love me,
Now spread Your wings above me
And shield me from alarm.
Though Satan would devour me,
Let angel guards sing o'er me:
This child of God shall meet no harm! Amen.

Preserve us, O Lord, while waking,
And guard us while sleeping;
That awake we may be with Christ
And in peace may take our rest. Amen.

*Antiphon from Compline*

## GRACE BEFORE MEALS

Come, Lord Jesus, be our Guest.
May this food by You be blest.
May our souls by You be fed
Always on Your living bread. Amen.

God bless this food and bless us all,
And keep us safe whate'er befall. Amen.

We thank You, Lord, for meat and drink,
Through Jesus Christ, our Lord. Amen.


## THANKS AFTER MEALS

Many, many thanks I say
For my food and drink today.
Father, all that hungry be,
Feed them as You're feeding me. Amen.

We thank You, Lord, for being near;
We thank You for our parents dear.
We thank You for the food we eat;
We thank You for Your name so sweet. Amen.

## GENERAL PRAYER

Jesus, help my eyes to see
All the good You're sending me.
Jesus, help my ears to hear
Calls for help from far and near.
Jesus, help my feet to go
In the way that You will show.
Jesus, help my hands to do
All things loving, kind, and true.
Jesus, help my body praise,
Serving You throughout my days. Amen.

## ON A BIRTHDAY

My years, dear Lord, are in Your keeping,
Each day comes, a gift from You.
This day I ask, Lord, in Your mercy,
Grant to me a year of blessing.
Serving You in grace and love,
Let my ev'ry thought and word,
My ev'ry deed, to You, be pleasing.
Help me be Your child, dear Lord.
Look down on me from heav'n above;
Bless me; touch me with Your love. Amen.

## ON THE WAY TO SCHOOL

I am but a little child—
Make my heart both pure and mild;
Thus a temple it shall be,
Dedicated, Lord, to Thee. Amen.

Holy Jesus, every day
Keep me in the narrow way;
And when earthly things are past,
Bring my ransomed soul at last
Where it needs no star to guide,
Where no clouds Your glory hide. Amen.

*William C. Dix, 1837–98, alt.*

## FOR PARENTS AND LOVED ONES

Hold them closely in Your keeping,
　　All the dear ones that I love;
Keep them safe, awake or sleeping,
　　Lord of earth and heaven above!
Guard them, oh, most tenderly;
They are safe, when kept by Thee. Amen.

## WHEN SICK

Tender Jesus, meek and mild,
Look on me a little child.
Help me, if it be Your will,
To recover from all ill. Amen.

## AT PLAY

Help me, Lord, to be today
Very kind in all my play;
Make me helpful, make me strong,
Show me what is right and wrong. Amen.

Jesus, Friend of little children,
Be a Friend to me;
Take my hand, and ever keep me
Always close to Thee. Amen.
*Walter J. Mathams, 1853–1931, alt.*

## PRAYER OF THANKSGIVING

Lord, bestow a grateful heart,
For the gifts You do impart
To a little child like me
Who depends alone on Thee. Amen.

# Books of the Bible

The Bible is divided into two parts, the Old Testament and the New Testament. There are 66 books in the Bible: 39 in the Old Testament and 27 in the New Testament.

# BOOKS OF THE OLD TESTAMENT

## Historical Books

Gen´e-sis
Ex´o-dus
Le-vit´i-cus
Num´bers
Deu-ter-on´o-my

*The Pen´ta-teuch* (The Five Books of Moses)

Josh´u-a
Judg´es
Ruth
First Sam´u-el
Second Sam´u-el
First Kings
Second Kings
First Chron´i-cles
Second Chron´i-cles
Ez´ra
Ne-he-mi´ah
Es´ther

## Poetic Books

Job
Psalms
Prov´erbs
Ec-cle-si-as´tes
    or The Preacher
Song of Sol´o-mon

## Prophetic Books
### *Major Prophets*

I-sa´iah
Jer-e-mi´ah
Lam-en-ta´tions
E-ze´kiel
Dan´iel

### *Minor Prophets*

Ho-se´a
Jo´el
A´mos
O-ba-di´ah
Jo´nah
Mi´cah

Na´hum
Hab-ak´kuk
Zeph-a-ni´ah
Hag´gai
Zech-a-ri´ah
Mal´a-chi

# BOOKS OF THE NEW TESTAMENT

**Matthew**

**Mark**

**Luke**

**John**

## Historical Books

Mat´thew
Mark
Luke
John
The Acts of the Apostles

## Epistles

Ro´mans
First Co-rin´thi-ans
Second Co-rin´thi-ans
Ga-la´tians
E-phe´sians
Phi-lip´pians
Co-los´sians
First Thes-sa-lo´nians
Second The-sa-lo´nians

First Tim´o-thy
Second Tim´o-thy
Ti´tus
Phi-le´mon
He´brews
James
First Pe´ter
Second Pe´ter
First John
Second John
Third John
Jude

## Prophetical Book

Rev-e-la´tion